Copyright © 2024 by VIRUTI SATYAN SHIVAN

All rights reserved. No part of this publication may be reproduced, stored in a retrieval system, or transmitted in any form or by any means, electronic, mechanical, photocopying, recording, or otherwise, without express written permission of the publisher, except in the case of brief quotations embodied in critical reviews and specific other noncommercial uses permitted by copyright law.

This book's characters, people, places, and events are fictitious. Any resemblance to natural persons, living or dead, or actual events or organizations is purely coincidental and not intended by the author.

White Coat Syndrome

-

The Comprehensive Guide

by

VIRUTI SHIVAN

Masters in Clinical Psychology (Major)

"In books, as in life, it's not the size or looks but the content that matters."

DISCLAIMER: The information in this book is provided for general informational purposes only and is not intended as professional advice. Although every effort has been made to ensure the accuracy and completeness of the information, the author and publisher do not assume responsibility for errors, inaccuracies, omissions, inconsistencies, or the impact of future advancements or updates in technology and information. This book is not a substitute for proper training, diagnosis, treatment, or guidance from qualified professionals. Readers are encouraged to consult experts in the relevant fields and independently verify the information when necessary. Any slights of people, places, or organizations are unintentional and purely coincidental.

Introduction	9
Chapter 1: Understanding White Coat Syndrome	**11**
1.1 The Psychology Behind White Coat Syndrome	11
1.2 Historical Perspectives on Patient Anxiety	13
1.3 The Impact of White Coat Syndrome on Health	16
1.4 Exercise: 10 MCQs with Answers at the End	18
Chapter 2: Symptoms and Recognition	**24**
2.1 Identifying Symptoms in Yourself and Others	24
2.2 Psychological vs. Physiological Symptoms	27
2.3 The Role of Awareness in Management	30
2.4 Exercise: 10 MCQs with Answers at the End	33
Chapter 3: The Role of Healthcare Professionals	**39**
3.1 Creating a Comforting Environment	39
3.2 Communication Strategies for Professionals	42
3.3 Patient-Centered Care Approaches	45
3.4 Exercise: 10 MCQs with Answers at the End	48
Chapter 4: Coping Mechanisms	**55**
4.1 Breathing Techniques for Immediate Relief	55
4.2 Cognitive Behavioral Therapy (CBT) Approaches	58
4.3 Long-Term Anxiety Management Strategies	61
4.4 Exercise: 10 MCQs with Answers at the End	64
Chapter 5: The Power of Preparation	**71**
5.1 Educating Yourself Before Appointments	71
5.2 The Checklist: What to Ask Your Doctor	74
5.3 Role-Playing and Scenario Planning	78
5.4 Exercise: 10 MCQs with Answers at the End	81
Chapter 6: Technological Aids and Mobile Apps	**87**
6.1 Apps for Meditation and Relaxation	87
6.2 Tracking Your Health Anxiety Trends	91

6.3 Virtual Reality Exposure Therapy	94
6.4 Exercise: 10 MCQs with Answers at the End	97
Chapter 7: Lifestyle Adjustments	**103**
7.1 Diet and Exercise	103
7.2 Sleep Hygiene and Its Impact on Anxiety	106
7.3 The Role of Social Support	109
7.4 Exercise: 10 MCQs with Answers at the End	112
Chapter 8: Understanding the Healthcare System	**117**
8.1 Navigating Healthcare Settings	117
8.2 Patient Rights and Advocacy	120
8.3 Building a Positive Relationship with Your Healthcare Provider	123
8.4 Exercise: 10 MCQs with Answers at the End	126
Chapter 9: Alternative Therapies	**131**
9.1 The Role of Acupuncture	131
9.2 Benefits of Massage Therapy	134
9.3 Herbal Supplements and Their Efficacy	137
9.4 Exercise: 10 MCQs with Answers at the End	140
Chapter 10: Children and White Coat Syndrome	**145**
10.1 Recognizing Signs in Children	145
10.2 Preparing a Child for a Doctor's Visit	148
10.3 Pediatric Care: Special Considerations	151
10.4 Exercise: 10 MCQs with Answers at the End	154
Chapter 11: The Future of Patient Care	**161**
11.1 Innovations in Reducing Patient Anxiety	161
11.2 The Role of Telemedicine	164
11.3 Personalized Medicine and Patient Comfort	167
11.4 Exercise: 10 MCQs with Answers at the End	170
Chapter 12: Case Studies and Success Stories	**175**
12.1 Overcoming Severe White Coat Syndrome	175

12.2 Innovative Approaches in Practice	178
12.3 Long-Term Management and Recovery	182
12.4 Exercise: 10 MCQs with Answers at the End	185
Chapter 13: Creating a Personal Action Plan	**191**
13.1 Setting Realistic Goals	191
13.2 Monitoring Progress and Adjusting Strategies	194
13.3 Utilizing Resources and Support Systems	197
13.4 Exercise: 10 MCQs with Answers at the End	200
Chapter 14: The Psychological Impact of Chronic Illness	**207**
14.1 Dealing with Diagnosis	207
14.2 Mental Health and Chronic Disease	210
14.3 Strategies for Emotional Resilience	213
14.4 Exercise: 10 MCQs with Answers at the End	217
Chapter 15: Preventative Strategies	**223**
15.1 Early Intervention Techniques	223
15.2 Education and Outreach Programs	226
15.3 Building a Culture of Understanding and Empathy in Healthcare	229
15.4 Exercise: 10 MCQs with Answers at the End	232
Conclusion	**237**

Introduction

Welcome to **"White Coat Syndrome - The Comprehensive Guide,"** a pivotal resource dedicated to understanding, managing, and overcoming the anxiety associated with medical environments. This guide is designed to serve as a beacon of hope and a tool of empowerment for those who find themselves grappling with the palpable tension that often accompanies visits to healthcare facilities.

White Coat Syndrome, characterized by heightened stress and anxiety in medical settings, affects a significant portion of the population. While the phenomenon is widely recognized, the pathways to navigating through this anxiety are less commonly understood. This book aims to bridge that gap, offering readers a deep dive into the psychological underpinnings of White Coat Syndrome alongside practical strategies for overcoming it.

Boldly confronting White Coat Syndrome requires an exploration of its roots, from the psychological triggers that exacerbate the condition to the societal and cultural factors that shape our experiences with healthcare. Through a combination of research-based insights and relatable anecdotes, we will embark on a journey to unpack the complexities of this syndrome. The objective is not only to inform but also to transform how individuals interact with the world of healthcare—turning experiences of dread into opportunities for growth and understanding.

As we delve into the chapters that follow, you will encounter a structured approach to tackling White Coat Syndrome. Each chapter is meticulously crafted to address different facets of the condition, from recognizing symptoms and understanding their causes to exploring coping mechanisms, both immediate and long-term. **Subchapters are designed to build on each other,** gradually equipping readers with the knowledge and tools necessary to face their anxieties with newfound confidence.

Importantly, this guide acknowledges the absence of visual aids. Instead, it leans on the power of words, narratives, and scenarios that resonate with the lived experiences of many. Through these stories, readers will find reflections on their fears and aspirations alongside strategies that have proven effective in real-world contexts.

In crafting this guide, special attention has been given to ensuring that the content is original, engaging, and, above all, helpful. The inclusion of personal anecdotes and hypothetical scenarios serves not only to illustrate critical points but also to enrich the narrative, making the journey through the book a relatable and transformative experience. By offering unique perspectives and innovative approaches to dealing with White Coat Syndrome, this book stands as a comprehensive resource for anyone looking to navigate the challenges of medical anxiety.

As we move forward, remember that this book is not just a collection of chapters but a pathway to empowerment. It's an invitation to explore, understand, and ultimately conquer the fears that accompany White Coat Syndrome. **Welcome to your journey towards a healthier, more confident you.**

Chapter 1: Understanding White Coat Syndrome

1.1 The Psychology Behind White Coat Syndrome

White Coat Syndrome, often marked by an increase in blood pressure readings and a surge of anxiety in medical settings, is a complex psychological phenomenon. It represents the intersection of physiological responses and psychological triggers when faced with healthcare environments or professionals. This subchapter delves into the intricate psychological underpinnings of White Coat Syndrome, unraveling the layers to understand why a simple medical appointment can evoke such a profound response.

At its core, **White Coat Syndrome** can be viewed through the lens of the fight-or-flight response, a primal reaction that occurs in the presence of perceived threats. In the context of a medical setting, the white coat becomes a symbol of potential discomfort, pain, or bad news, triggering this innate response. The anticipation of an encounter with healthcare professionals can activate stress hormones, leading to measurable physical symptoms such as increased heart rate and blood pressure.

The role of past experiences cannot be overstated in shaping one's reaction to medical environments. Individuals with previous negative healthcare encounters, be it through personal experiences or those of close others, are more likely to develop White Coat Syndrome. These memories, whether conscious or subconscious, contribute to the anxiety felt during subsequent visits, creating a cycle of fear and avoidance.

Cultural and societal influences also play a pivotal role. The portrayal of medical procedures in media, stories shared within communities, and the general perception of healthcare can all influence one's psychological response to medical environments. In some cases, societal stigma associated with certain medical conditions can exacerbate the anxiety related to healthcare visits.

Understanding White Coat Syndrome also involves acknowledging the **individual differences** in anxiety thresholds and coping mechanisms. While some may find medical settings mildly uncomfortable, others may experience overwhelming anxiety. This variability is influenced by factors such as personality traits, coping styles, and the presence of underlying anxiety disorders.

Psychological theories offer further insight into White Coat Syndrome. For instance, **conditioning theories** suggest that if a person has been conditioned to associate medical settings with adverse outcomes, the mere anticipation of a medical encounter can trigger anxiety. On the other hand, **cognitive-behavioral theories** focus on how negative thought patterns and beliefs about healthcare can fuel fear and avoidance behaviors.

To combat White Coat Syndrome, it is crucial to employ strategies that address both the psychological triggers and the physiological responses. Techniques such as cognitive-behavioral therapy (CBT), mindfulness, and exposure therapy can be effective in altering the negative perceptions and reactions associated with medical settings. Additionally, fostering positive healthcare experiences and building trust with healthcare providers can gradually diminish the power of White Coat Syndrome.

In summary, the psychology behind White Coat Syndrome is multifaceted, rooted in a combination of evolutionary responses, personal history, cultural influences, and individual psychological makeup. Understanding these factors is the first step towards developing effective strategies to manage and overcome the anxiety associated with medical environments. Through this knowledge, individuals can embark on a path towards more positive healthcare experiences marked by less fear and more empowerment.

1.2 Historical Perspectives on Patient Anxiety

The phenomenon of patient anxiety, particularly in the guise of White Coat Syndrome, is not a modern-day construct but has historical roots that stretch back through the annals of medical history. This subchapter explores the evolution of patient anxiety, shedding light on how historical developments in healthcare and societal attitudes towards medicine have shaped the current understanding and experiences of medical-related stress.

Historically, **the relationship between healthcare providers and patients** was starkly different from today's standards. In ancient and medieval times, medical practices were intertwined with mysticism and the supernatural, often leaving patients in a state of fear and uncertainty. The unpredictability of treatments, coupled with a lack of understanding of medical conditions, contributed to a baseline level of anxiety around healthcare.

As medical science advanced through the Renaissance and into the modern era, the establishment of hospitals and the professionalization of the medical field brought about significant changes. However, these developments also introduced new sources of patient anxiety. **The clinical environment of hospitals**, with their stark, impersonal settings and the emergence of surgeries and invasive procedures, heightened fears about medical interventions. The white coat, adopted in the late 19th and early 20th centuries as a symbol of cleanliness and professionalism, also became an accidental symbol of fear for many.

The **20th century** saw a paradigm shift with the advent of patient rights and the movement toward patient-centered care. Despite these advances, patient anxiety remained a significant issue, influenced by the rapid pace of medical innovations and the often impersonal nature of healthcare delivery. The increased specialization within medicine, while improving treatment outcomes, also led to a fragmentation of care that could be disorienting and anxiety-provoking for patients.

Societal attitudes towards illness and healthcare have also played a role in shaping patient anxiety. Historical stigmatization of certain diseases, combined with a lack of public knowledge about health and medicine, has contributed to fears around diagnosis and treatment. The development of the healthcare system, with its complexities and bureaucracies, has introduced additional stressors, including concerns about accessibility, affordability, and the quality of care.

In recent decades, the **digital revolution** has transformed access to medical information. While this has empowered some patients, it has also led to the phenomenon of cyberchondria, where easy access to health information online exacerbates health-related anxieties. The abundance of information—both accurate and misleading—can overwhelm patients, leading to increased anxiety rather than reassurance.

The historical perspectives on patient anxiety reveal a complex interplay between medical advancements, societal attitudes, and the evolution of the doctor-patient relationship. Understanding this history is crucial for addressing modern-day manifestations of patient anxiety, such as White Coat Syndrome. It highlights the importance of continuing to evolve healthcare practices towards more empathetic, patient-centered approaches that recognize and mitigate the deep-rooted anxieties patients may face. This historical context underscores the need for healthcare systems to not only advance medically but also to evolve in ways that address the psychological well-being of patients, acknowledging the historical legacies that continue to shape patient experiences today.

1.3 The Impact of White Coat Syndrome on Health

White Coat Syndrome, characterized by elevated blood pressure readings in a clinical setting, extends its impact beyond mere numbers on a blood pressure monitor. This syndrome encapsulates a broader spectrum of health implications, affecting both the psychological well-being and the physical health of individuals. This subchapter delves into the multifaceted impact of White Coat Syndrome on health, highlighting the importance of recognizing and addressing this condition not just as a curious phenomenon but as a significant health concern.

Psychological Impact: At its core, White Coat Syndrome is rooted in anxiety and stress, which can have profound effects on an individual's mental health. The fear of medical environments can lead to chronic stress, which is known to contribute to a host of psychological issues, including anxiety disorders, depression, and sleep disturbances. The anticipatory anxiety associated with healthcare visits can also exacerbate existing mental health conditions, creating a vicious cycle of fear and healthcare avoidance.

Physical Health Consequences: Beyond its psychological ramifications, White Coat Syndrome can obscure the accurate diagnosis and management of hypertension. Individuals with this syndrome may present with elevated blood pressure readings in clinical settings while having regular readings at home. This discrepancy can lead to misdiagnosis, over-treatment, or under-treatment of hypertension, potentially resulting in inappropriate medication adjustments and increased risk of cardiovascular disease. Conversely, the stress-induced spikes in blood pressure can also have real, albeit temporary, effects on cardiovascular health, increasing the risk of stroke, heart attack, and other stress-related conditions over time.

Healthcare Utilization and Avoidance: One of the most concerning impacts of White Coat Syndrome is the potential for healthcare avoidance. Individuals who experience significant anxiety in medical settings may postpone or avoid necessary medical appointments, screenings, and treatments. This avoidance behavior can delay the diagnosis and treatment of potentially serious conditions, leading to worse health outcomes. Moreover, the reluctance to engage with healthcare providers can undermine the effectiveness of patient-provider communication, hindering the development of a therapeutic alliance that is crucial for effective healthcare delivery.

Impact on Lifestyle and Health Behaviors: White Coat Syndrome may also influence an individual's health behaviors outside the clinical setting. The stress associated with medical visits can lead to unhealthy coping mechanisms, such as smoking, excessive alcohol consumption, or poor dietary choices. Additionally, the fear of receiving negative health feedback can discourage individuals from monitoring their health or engaging in preventive health behaviors, such as regular exercise or health screenings.

Addressing the Impact: Recognizing and addressing White Coat Syndrome is essential for mitigating its adverse effects on health. Healthcare providers can play a pivotal role by creating a more welcoming and less intimidating clinical environment, employing techniques to reduce patient anxiety, and considering home blood pressure monitoring for individuals affected by this syndrome. Moreover, educating patients about the nature of White Coat Syndrome and offering support for anxiety management can empower patients to take proactive steps toward improving their healthcare experiences.

In summary, the impact of White Coat Syndrome on health is significant and multifaceted, affecting psychological well-being, physical health, healthcare utilization, and lifestyle. By understanding the breadth of its implications, healthcare professionals and patients alike can work together to minimize its effects, ensuring more accurate healthcare assessments and promoting better overall health outcomes.

1.4 Exercise: 10 MCQs with Answers at the End

This exercise is designed to reinforce your understanding of the concepts covered in the first chapter of "Understanding White Coat Syndrome." Below are multiple-choice questions (MCQs) that encompass critical points from the chapter. Following the questions, you will find the answers to check your understanding.

Questions:

1. What is the primary psychological mechanism behind White Coat Syndrome?

   A. Happiness

   B. Stress and anxiety

   C. Excitement

   D. Indifference

2. Which of the following historical medical practices were often associated with?

   A. High levels of patient trust

   B. Mysticism and the supernatural

   C. Advanced technology

   D. None of the above

3. Which of the following best describes the impact of White Coat Syndrome on diagnoses?

   A. It has no impact on diagnoses.

   B. It can lead to under-treatment of hypertension.

C. It ensures more accurate diagnoses.

D. It is beneficial for diagnosing unrelated conditions.

4. How does chronic stress, related to White Coat Syndrome, affect mental health?

　A. Improves cognitive function

　B. Has no effect

　C. May contribute to anxiety disorders and depression

　D. Enhances mood stability

5. What role do past medical experiences play in White Coat Syndrome?

　A. No role

　B. They can exacerbate the condition.

　C. They reduce the syndrome's effects.

　D. They change the color preference for coats.

6. Which strategy is NOT recommended for managing White Coat Syndrome?

　A. Avoiding all future medical appointments

　B. Employing relaxation techniques before appointments

　C. Using home blood pressure monitoring

　D. Building a positive relationship with healthcare providers

7. Which behavior can the anticipatory anxiety of healthcare visits lead to?

   A. Increased frequency of visits

   B. Healthcare avoidance

   C. Enhanced communication with healthcare providers

   D. Improved health outcomes

8. White Coat Syndrome can result in mismanagement of which condition?

   A. Asthma

   B. Hypertension

   C. Diabetes

   D. None of the above

9. Cultural and societal influences on White Coat Syndrome include all EXCEPT:

   A. Portrayal of medical procedures in media

   B. Personal health practices and diet

   C. Stories shared within communities

   D. General perception of healthcare

10. Effective communication with healthcare providers is crucial for:

   A. Increasing anxiety

   B. Misdiagnosing conditions

   C. Overcoming White Coat Syndrome

   D. Avoiding medical care altogether

Answers:

1. B. Stress and anxiety

2. B. Mysticism and the supernatural

3. B. It can lead to under-treatment of hypertension.

4. C. May contribute to anxiety disorders and depression

5. B. They can exacerbate the condition.

6. A. Avoiding all future medical appointments

7. B. Healthcare avoidance

8. B. Hypertension

9. B. Personal health practices and diet

10. C. Overcoming White Coat Syndrome

These questions and answers are designed to test your comprehension of White Coat Syndrome, including its psychological underpinnings, historical perspectives, impacts on health, and strategies for management. Understanding these concepts is crucial for both patients and healthcare professionals in navigating and addressing the challenges associated with this condition.

Chapter 2: Symptoms and Recognition

2.1 Identifying Symptoms in Yourself and Others

Recognizing the symptoms of White Coat Syndrome is the first step towards addressing and managing this condition effectively. It's essential to understand that while the primary manifestation of this syndrome is elevated blood pressure readings in a clinical setting, there are several other psychological and physiological symptoms associated with it. This subchapter aims to equip you with the knowledge to identify these symptoms in yourself and others, fostering a proactive approach to healthcare and well-being.

Psychological Symptoms:

- **Anxiety and Nervousness:** One of the most common indicators of White Coat Syndrome is a noticeable increase in anxiety or nervousness leading up to or during a medical appointment. This may manifest as restlessness, a sense of dread, or overwhelming worry about the visit.

- **Fear of Medical Settings:** A distinct fear or discomfort when thinking about or being in medical environments, even if the visit is for a routine check-up or unrelated to the individual's health concerns.

- **Stress-Induced Symptoms:** Symptoms such as headaches, dizziness, or nausea that specifically arise in anticipation of or during medical encounters can also be indicative of White Coat Syndrome.

Physiological Symptoms:

- **Elevated Blood Pressure Readings:** The hallmark of White Coat Syndrome, where blood pressure readings are significantly higher in clinical settings compared to at home or in other non-medical environments.

- **Increased Heart Rate:** A noticeable increase in heart rate or palpitations when in a medical setting or thinking about a medical visit.

- **Sweating and Trembling:** Physical manifestations of anxiety, such as sweating or trembling, may occur during a medical appointment or in anticipation of one.

Behavioral Symptoms:

- **Healthcare Avoidance:** Delaying or avoiding medical appointments, screenings, or treatments due to anxiety and fear associated with medical settings.

- **Difficulty Communicating with Healthcare Providers:** Anxiety may lead to trouble articulating questions, concerns, or symptoms to healthcare professionals, hindering effective communication and care.

- **Overpreparation or Rehearsal:** Some individuals may overprepare for appointments or rehearse conversations due to anxiety as a way to gain control over the situation.

Recognition in Others:

Identifying White Coat Syndrome in others requires attentiveness to both verbal cues and non-verbal behaviors. Listen for expressions of dread or anxiety related to medical visits and observe for signs of distress, such as avoidance of healthcare discussions, physical discomfort when in medical settings, or reluctance to schedule or attend medical appointments.

Understanding and empathy are crucial when recognizing symptoms of White Coat Syndrome in others. Offering support, sharing information about the condition, and encouraging conversations about health-related anxieties can make a significant difference in how individuals approach their healthcare needs.

In summary, identifying the symptoms of White Coat Syndrome involves a holistic view of the individual's psychological, physiological, and behavioral responses to medical settings. By recognizing these signs in ourselves and others, we can take meaningful steps towards managing the syndrome effectively, ensuring that healthcare experiences are as positive and productive as possible.

2.2 Psychological vs. Physiological Symptoms

Understanding White Coat Syndrome requires differentiating between its psychological and physiological symptoms. This distinction is critical not only for recognizing the syndrome but also for devising effective strategies to manage it. Here, we explore the nuances between these two categories of symptoms, shedding light on how they manifest and intersect in the context of White Coat Syndrome.

Psychological Symptoms:

Psychological symptoms are primarily related to the emotional and cognitive responses individuals experience in anticipation of or during medical appointments. These symptoms include:

- **Anxiety and Fear:** The anticipation of medical procedures or receiving health news can provoke intense feelings of anxiety and fear, often disproportionate to the actual situation.

- **Stress:** The stress associated with medical environments can trigger a range of emotional responses, from mild unease to severe panic, affecting one's mental well-being.

- **Avoidance Behavior:** A psychological symptom that leads to postponing or skipping medical appointments due to the fear and anxiety they evoke.

- **Cognitive Distortions:** Negative thinking patterns, such as catastrophizing or overgeneralizing about medical procedures and outcomes, are common psychological symptoms.

Physiological Symptoms:

Physiological symptoms of White Coat Syndrome are the physical manifestations of the body's response to stress and anxiety. These include:

- **Elevated Blood Pressure:** The most recognized physiological symptom where an individual's blood pressure spikes in a clinical setting.

- **Increased Heart Rate:** Anxiety and stress can lead to palpitations or an accelerated heart rate, often noticed during medical examinations.

- **Sweating:** Nervousness and anxiety can cause excessive sweating, particularly in the palms, forehead, and underarms.

- **Tremors:** Fine shakes or tremors, especially in the hands, may occur due to the nervous system's response to stress.

Interconnection Between Psychological and Physiological Symptoms:

The psychological and physiological symptoms of White Coat Syndrome are deeply interconnected. Psychological stress triggers the body's fight-or-flight response, leading to the release of stress hormones such as adrenaline and cortisol. These hormones are responsible for the physiological symptoms observed, including elevated blood pressure and increased heart rate. Conversely, experiencing these physiological symptoms can heighten psychological distress, creating a feedback loop that exacerbates the syndrome.

Recognizing the Interplay:

Effective management of White Coat Syndrome involves addressing both the psychological and physiological aspects of the condition. Recognizing the interplay between these symptoms is crucial for healthcare providers and patients alike. For instance, employing relaxation techniques or cognitive-behavioral strategies can help mitigate psychological symptoms, which in turn can reduce the physiological manifestations of the syndrome. Conversely, monitoring physiological symptoms through home blood pressure measurements or biofeedback can provide reassurance and alleviate psychological stress.

In summary, distinguishing between the psychological and physiological symptoms of White Coat Syndrome is essential for understanding its complexity. By acknowledging the interconnected nature of these symptoms, individuals and healthcare professionals can work together to develop comprehensive strategies that address the syndrome holistically, leading to improved health outcomes and more positive healthcare experiences.

2.3 The Role of Awareness in Management

Awareness plays a pivotal role in the effective management of White Coat Syndrome, serving as the foundation upon which strategies for coping and treatment are built. Understanding the syndrome's manifestations, triggers, and impacts can empower individuals to take proactive steps toward mitigation. This subchapter explores how increased awareness—both on the part of patients and healthcare providers—can significantly influence the management of White Coat Syndrome.

Patient Awareness:

For patients, developing an awareness of White Coat Syndrome involves recognizing its symptoms, understanding its triggers, and acknowledging its potential impact on health outcomes. This level of self-awareness enables individuals to:

- **Identify Personal Triggers:** Understanding what aspects of medical environments or procedures trigger anxiety can help patients develop targeted coping strategies.

- **Seek Appropriate Support:** Armed with awareness, patients are better positioned to seek out resources, whether that involves consulting healthcare professionals, exploring relaxation techniques, or joining support groups.

- **Implement Self-Monitoring Practices:** Awareness encourages patients to adopt practices like home blood pressure monitoring, which can provide a more accurate reflection of their health status away from the stress-inducing clinical environment.

Healthcare Provider Awareness:

Healthcare professionals play a crucial role in the management of White Coat Syndrome, and their awareness of the condition can significantly affect patient care. This includes:

- **Recognizing Symptoms:** Providers trained to recognize the signs of White Coat Syndrome can take steps to alleviate patient anxiety, such as engaging in more empathetic communication or offering a more relaxed environment for blood pressure measurements.

- **Adopting Patient-Centered Approaches:** Awareness of the syndrome encourages healthcare providers to adopt strategies that prioritize patient comfort and involvement in care decisions, fostering a more trusting and supportive doctor-patient relationship.

- **Educating Patients:** By informing patients about White Coat Syndrome, healthcare providers can demystify the condition, helping patients understand that their elevated blood pressure readings in clinical settings may not necessarily indicate hypertension.

Joint Awareness and Communication:

The synergy between patient and healthcare provider awareness can enhance the management of White Coat Syndrome. Open communication about the condition can lead to more accurate health assessments and tailored treatment plans. For instance, discussing home blood pressure monitoring results can provide a more comprehensive picture of a patient's cardiovascular health, leading to more informed treatment decisions.

Awareness as a Tool for Empowerment:

Ultimately, awareness acts as a tool for empowerment, enabling both patients and healthcare providers to confront White Coat Syndrome more effectively. It allows for the identification of specific needs and preferences, the customization of management strategies, and the fostering of a collaborative approach to healthcare. By elevating awareness, individuals can transform their relationship with healthcare settings from one of anxiety and avoidance to one of engagement and proactive health management.

In summary, the role of awareness in the management of White Coat Syndrome is multifaceted and essential. It empowers patients to take control of their healthcare experiences and encourages healthcare providers to adopt practices that reduce anxiety and improve patient outcomes. Through increased awareness and collaboration, the cycle of fear and avoidance associated with White Coat Syndrome can be broken, leading to healthier and more positive healthcare experiences.

2.4 Exercise: 10 MCQs with Answers at the End

Test your understanding of the concepts covered in Chapter 2: "Symptoms and Recognition," with the following multiple-choice questions. These questions are designed to reinforce your knowledge about identifying symptoms of White Coat Syndrome, distinguishing between psychological and physiological symptoms, understanding the role of awareness in management, and more.

Questions:

1. Which of the following is a psychological symptom of White Coat Syndrome?

   A. Elevated blood pressure

   B. Increased heart rate

   C. Anxiety and fear

   D. Sweating

2. A physiological response to White Coat Syndrome includes:

   A. Avoidance behavior

   B. Cognitive distortions

   C. Tremors

   D. Stress-induced symptoms

3. Recognizing White Coat Syndrome symptoms in others can be facilitated by:

   A. Ignoring verbal cues

   B. Observing non-verbal behaviors

   C. Focusing solely on physiological symptoms

   D. Assuming everyone experiences the syndrome in the same way

4. The primary trigger of White Coat Syndrome is:

   A. Lack of exercise

   B. The clinical environment

   C. Poor diet

   D. Insufficient sleep

5. Which is NOT a recommended strategy for managing White Coat Syndrome?

   A. Healthcare avoidance

   B. Relaxation techniques before appointments

   C. Home blood pressure monitoring

   D. Effective communication with healthcare providers

6. Patient awareness in managing White Coat Syndrome involves:

   A. Recognizing personal triggers

   B. Seeking inappropriate support

   C. Avoiding all medical information

   D. Ignoring symptoms

7. Healthcare provider awareness affects patient care by:

   A. Decreasing the accuracy of health assessments

   B. Adopting patient-centered approaches

   C. Discouraging patients from discussing their fears

   D. Overlooking symptoms of White Coat Syndrome

8. The impact of awareness on the management of White Coat Syndrome includes:

   A. Increased patient and provider frustration

   B. Enhanced joint communication and treatment planning

   C. Reduced emphasis on patient comfort

   D. Limiting patient involvement in care decisions

9. Effective management of White Coat Syndrome requires:

   A. Focusing on physiological symptoms only

   B. Ignoring psychological symptoms

   C. Addressing both psychological and physiological symptoms

   D. Avoiding discussions about the syndrome

10. The role of patient-provider communication in managing White Coat Syndrome is to:

    A. Confirm biases and fears

    B. Encourage avoidance behaviors

    C. Facilitate more accurate health assessments

    D. Increase anxiety through misinformation

Answers:

1. C. Anxiety and fear
2. C. Tremors
3. B. Observing non-verbal behaviors
4. B. The clinical environment
5. A. Healthcare avoidance
6. A. Recognizing personal triggers
7. B. Adopting patient-centered approaches
8. B. Enhanced joint communication and treatment planning
9. C. Addressing both psychological and physiological symptoms
10. C. Facilitate more accurate health assessments

These questions are designed to help you reflect on the critical points discussed in Chapter 2 and deepen your understanding of how to identify and manage White Coat Syndrome effectively.

Chapter 3: The Role of Healthcare Professionals

3.1 Creating a Comforting Environment

Healthcare professionals play a crucial role in mitigating the effects of White Coat Syndrome, with the creation of a comforting environment being a fundamental aspect of patient care. A welcoming and reassuring atmosphere can significantly reduce the anxiety and stress associated with medical visits, thereby improving the overall patient experience and the accuracy of medical assessments. This subchapter outlines strategies healthcare providers can employ to foster a calming environment, emphasizing the importance of empathy, communication, and patient-centered care.

Physical Environment Adjustments:

- **Warm and Inviting Spaces:** Transitioning from sterile, impersonal spaces to warmer, more inviting environments can have a profound impact on patient comfort. Consider the use of softer lighting, comfortable seating, and calming colors in waiting areas and examination rooms.

- **Privacy and Respect:** Ensuring that conversations and examinations are conducted in private spaces can help patients feel secure and respected, reducing stress levels and fostering trust.

- **Accessible Information:** Providing clear, accessible information about procedures, what to expect during the visit, and health resources can empower patients and alleviate fears of the unknown.

Communication Techniques:

- **Active Listening:** Show patients that their concerns and feelings are valid through active listening. This involves making eye contact, nodding, and responding appropriately to their problems, which can help patients feel heard and valued.

- **Clear and Compassionate Communication:** Use language that is easy to understand, avoiding medical jargon that may confuse or intimidate patients. Express empathy and understanding for their feelings and concerns.

- **Encourage Questions:** Make it clear that patients are encouraged to ask questions about their care, concerns, and any aspect of their health. A proactive approach to inviting questions can demystify the healthcare experience and reduce anxiety.

Procedure and Interaction Modifications:

- **Explain Procedures:** Before performing any procedures, explain what will be done, why it's necessary, and what the patient can expect to feel. This transparency can help reduce fear of the unknown.

- **Patient Control:** Where possible, give patients control over aspects of their care. This could be as simple as asking for their preference on where to sit or offering them a choice in appointment times.

- **Gentle and Reassuring Touch:** When appropriate, a gentle touch can be reassuring to patients, conveying compassion and care.

Building a Supportive Atmosphere:

- **Staff Training:** Train all staff members, from receptionists to nurses and doctors, on the importance of creating a welcoming environment. The attitudes and behaviors of staff can significantly influence a patient's comfort level.

- **Follow-Up:** Consider follow-up calls or messages to check on patients after their visit, mainly if they exhibited signs of anxiety or distress. This shows that their well-being is a priority beyond the immediate scope of the visit.

- **Feedback Mechanisms:** Implement mechanisms for patients to provide feedback on their experience. This not only allows for continuous improvement but also gives patients a voice in their care.

Creating a comforting environment is a multi-faceted approach that encompasses the physical setting, communication strategies, and the overall atmosphere of the healthcare setting. By prioritizing these elements, healthcare professionals can play a significant role in reducing White Coat Syndrome, leading to better health outcomes and a more positive healthcare experience for patients. This approach not only benefits those with White Coat Syndrome but enhances the quality of care for all patients, reinforcing the importance of empathy, respect, and patient-centered practices in healthcare.

3.2 Communication Strategies for Professionals

Effective communication is a cornerstone of patient care, particularly for individuals experiencing White Coat Syndrome. Healthcare professionals can significantly alleviate patient anxiety and improve outcomes through thoughtful, clear, and empathetic communication. This subchapter delves into specific strategies healthcare providers can employ to enhance their communication with patients, aiming to build trust, reduce anxiety, and foster a collaborative care environment.

Establishing Rapport:

- **Personal Greetings:** Begin interactions with a personal greeting and use the patient's name. This simple act can make patients feel seen and valued as individuals, not just as another appointment on the schedule.

- **Non-Verbal Cues:** Pay attention to non-verbal cues such as body language and eye contact. A friendly posture and direct eye contact can convey openness and willingness to listen, creating a more inviting atmosphere for the patient.

- **Show Empathy:** Demonstrate empathy through verbal affirmations and acknowledgments of the patient's feelings. Phrases like "I understand why that might be worrying" can validate their emotions and reduce feelings of isolation.

Simplifying Medical Information:

- **Avoid Jargon:** Use layperson's terms when discussing diagnoses, procedures, and treatments. Complex medical terminology can confuse and intimidate patients, exacerbating their anxiety.

- **Use Visual Aids:** When possible, use diagrams, models, or digital visuals to explain conditions or procedures. Visual aids can help patients better understand their health and the care they are receiving.

- **Provide Written Summaries:** Offering written summaries of key points discussed during the appointment can help patients remember and process information at their own pace.

Encouraging Patient Participation:

- **Ask Open-Ended Questions:** Encourage patients to share their thoughts and concerns by asking open-ended questions. This invites more detailed responses and signals that their input is valued.

- **Active Listening:** Practice active listening by focusing intently on the patient's words, summarizing their points for clarity, and responding thoughtfully. This demonstrates respect for their perspective and aids in addressing their concerns accurately.

- **Empower Decision-Making:** Whenever possible, involve patients in decision-making about their care. Discuss options openly, including the benefits and risks of each, to empower patients to make informed choices.

Handling Anxiety and Concerns:

- **Acknowledge Anxiety:** Directly acknowledging a patient's anxiety can be the first step in alleviating it. Recognize their feelings and discuss strategies or adjustments that could make them more comfortable.

- **Provide Reassurance:** Offer reassurance about the procedures or treatments being recommended. Highlighting the benefits and addressing common fears can help reduce anxiety.

- **Follow-Up:** Implement a system for follow-up communication, allowing patients to ask questions or express concerns that arise after they leave the office. This ongoing support can significantly impact their comfort and compliance with treatment plans.

Feedback and Continuous Improvement:

- **Solicit Feedback:** Regularly ask patients for feedback on their experience and communication preferences. This not only improves the quality of care but also reinforces to patients that their opinions are valued and considered.

- **Reflect and Adjust:** Reflect on patient interactions to identify areas for improvement. Continuous learning and adjustment of communication strategies can enhance patient relationships and care outcomes over time.

By adopting these communication strategies, healthcare professionals can significantly mitigate the impact of White Coat Syndrome and improve the healthcare experience for all patients. Effective communication fosters a therapeutic relationship built on trust, understanding, and mutual respect, essential components of quality patient care.

3.3 Patient-Centered Care Approaches

Patient-centered care is a holistic approach that places the patient at the core of healthcare decisions and practices. It emphasizes the importance of considering patients' preferences, needs, and values and ensures that patient values guide all clinical decisions. For individuals experiencing White Coat Syndrome, patient-centered care can be particularly effective in alleviating anxiety and enhancing the overall healthcare experience. This subchapter explores various patient-centered care approaches that healthcare professionals can adopt to support patients more effectively.

Respecting Patient Preferences:

- **Individualized Care Plans:** Develop care plans that are tailored to each patient's specific needs, preferences, and values. This involves engaging in detailed conversations with patients about their health goals and concerns.

- **Flexible Scheduling:** Offer flexible scheduling options to accommodate patients' personal and work lives, reducing stress associated with making and attending appointments.

- **Comfort Choices:** Allow patients to make small choices about their care environment, such as the temperature of the room or the selection of background music during examinations, to give them a sense of control.

Enhancing Communication:

- **Collaborative Dialogue:** Foster a two-way dialogue where patients feel comfortable voicing their thoughts, questions, and concerns. Ensure that communication is not just informative but also collaborative, enabling patients to participate in their care actively.

- **Transparency:** Be transparent about all aspects of care, including treatment options, potential side effects, and costs. This openness helps build trust and empowers patients to make informed decisions.

- **Cultural Competence:** Cultivate cultural competence among healthcare staff to ensure that care is sensitive and responsive to the diverse backgrounds and needs of patients. This includes understanding and respecting cultural, familial, and religious influences on health decisions.

Involving Patients in Decision Making:

- **Shared Decision-Making:** Implement shared decision-making practices, where healthcare providers and patients work together to make decisions about treatments and care plans. This approach respects patients' autonomy and acknowledges their expertise in their own lives and experiences.

- **Informed Consent:** Ensure that informed consent is truly knowledgeable, providing patients with all the information they need to understand the implications of treatment decisions fully.

- **Patient Education:** Offer educational resources and programs tailored to patients' literacy levels and learning preferences, enabling them to gain a deeper understanding of their health conditions and the rationale behind recommended treatments.

Support Beyond Clinical Care:

- **Emotional Support:** Recognize the emotional and psychological aspects of patient care. Provide support through counseling services, support groups, or referrals to mental health professionals as needed.

- **Social Support:** Connect patients with community resources and support networks that can assist with non-medical aspects of their health, such as transportation, housing, or nutrition.

- **Follow-Up Care:** Establish a systematic approach to follow-up care, ensuring that patients receive ongoing support and monitoring after initial treatments. This can include regular check-ins, remote monitoring, or coordination with other healthcare providers.

Adopting patient-centered care approaches requires a shift in mindset from healthcare providers, moving away from a purely biomedical model to one that sees patients as partners in care. By focusing on respect, empathy, and collaboration, healthcare professionals can create a more compassionate, responsive, and adequate healthcare environment. This not only improves outcomes for individuals with White Coat Syndrome but also enhances the quality of care for all patients, leading to more satisfying healthcare experiences and better overall health outcomes.

3.4 Exercise: 10 MCQs with Answers at the End

This exercise is designed to reinforce your understanding of the concepts covered in Chapter 3: "The Role of Healthcare Professionals," focusing on creating a comforting environment, communication strategies, and patient-centered care approaches. These multiple-choice questions will help you review and consolidate your knowledge.

Questions:

1. What is the primary goal of patient-centered care?

    A. To increase the efficiency of healthcare services

    B. To prioritize the patient's preferences, needs, and values in care decisions

    C. To reduce healthcare costs

    D. To enhance the reputation of healthcare facilities

2. Which strategy helps create a comforting environment for patients?

    A. Using bright, fluorescent lighting

    B. Offering flexible scheduling options

    C. Limiting patient choices in their care

    D. Avoiding the use of visual aids

3. Effective communication in patient-centered care involves:

    A. Using medical jargon to demonstrate expertise

    B. Encouraging a one-way dialogue where the healthcare professional does most of the talking

    C. Active listening and responding to patient concerns

    D. Providing minimal information to avoid overwhelming the patient

4. The practice of shared decision-making is characterized by:

   A. Healthcare professionals making decisions on behalf of the patient

   B. Patients making all decisions without input from healthcare professionals

   C. Healthcare professionals and patients working together to make decisions

   D. Delegating decision-making to family members

5. Which of the following is NOT a component of creating a comforting environment?

   A. Private and respectful interactions

   B. Personalized greeting using the patient's name

   C. Rushed consultations to reduce wait times for other patients

   D. Comfort choices, like room temperature adjustments

6. Tailoring healthcare communications to be culturally competent involves:

   A. Assuming all patients share similar cultural backgrounds

   B. Ignoring cultural differences to avoid stereotyping

   C. Recognizing and respecting diverse cultural influences on health decisions

   D. Focusing solely on clinical outcomes without considering cultural context

7. In patient-centered care, patient education is essential because it:

   A. Allows healthcare professionals to spend less time with each patient

   B. Enables patients to make informed decisions about their care

   C. Discourages patients from asking too many questions

   D. Shifts responsibility for care outcomes solely to the patient

8. an essential aspect of enhancing communication with patients is:

   A. Limiting the time spent on each consultation

   B. Avoiding discussions about patient fears and anxieties

   C. Using visual aids and written summaries to clarify information

   D. Encouraging patients to rely on online resources instead of asking questions

9. Providing emotional support to patients as part of patient-centered care may include:

   A. Discouraging expression of emotions to maintain a professional atmosphere

   B. Referring patients to counseling services or support groups

   C. Telling patients that anxiety and stress are normal and to be expected

D. Focusing exclusively on physical symptoms without addressing emotional needs

10. Flexibility in scheduling and care options is crucial because it:

   A. Ensures that healthcare professionals' time is maximized

   B. Reduces the need for patient feedback and customization of care

   C. Helps accommodate patients' personal and work lives, reducing stress

   D. Allows healthcare facilities to standardize care for all patients

Answers:

1. B. To prioritize the patient's preferences, needs, and values in care decisions

2. B. Offering flexible scheduling options

3. C. Active listening and responding to patient concerns

4. C. Healthcare professionals and patients working together to make decisions

5. C. Rushed consultations to reduce wait times for other patients

6. C. Recognizing and respecting diverse cultural influences on health decisions

7. B. Enables patients to make informed decisions about their care

8. C. Using visual aids and written summaries to clarify information

9. B. Referring patients to counseling services or support groups

10. C. Helps accommodate patients' personal and work lives, reducing stress

These questions are designed to test your understanding of the principles and practices of patient-centered care, emphasizing the importance of communication, respect for patient preferences, and the provision of supportive care environments.

Chapter 4: Coping Mechanisms

4.1 Breathing Techniques for Immediate Relief

Breathing techniques are a powerful tool for managing anxiety and stress, including the discomfort experienced due to White Coat Syndrome. These techniques can offer immediate relief by activating the body's natural relaxation response, helping to lower blood pressure, reduce heart rate, and calm the nervous system. This subchapter introduces several practical breathing exercises that patients can use to alleviate anxiety in medical settings or anticipation of healthcare visits.

Diaphragmatic Breathing (Belly Breathing):

- **Technique:** Sit or lie down comfortably, placing one hand on your belly and the other on your chest. Inhale slowly and deeply through your nose, allowing your belly to rise more than your chest. Exhale slowly through your mouth, gently contracting your abdominal muscles to empty your lungs.

- **Benefits:** Diaphragmatic breathing encourages full oxygen exchange and can help decrease the heart rate and blood pressure, promoting physical and mental relaxation.

4-7-8 Breathing:

- **Technique:** Begin by exhaling completely through your mouth. Close your mouth and inhale quietly through your nose to a mental count of four. Hold your breath for a count of seven. Exhale completely through your mouth to a count of eight. This is one cycle. Repeat the cycle three more times for a total of four breaths.

- **Benefits:** The 4-7-8 breathing technique can help reduce anxiety by increasing the concentration of oxygen in your blood, slowing your heart rate, and promoting a state of calm.

Box Breathing (Square Breathing):

- **Technique:** Inhale slowly to a count of four. Hold your breath for a count of four. Exhale slowly through your mouth to a count of four. Hold the exhalation for a count of four. This forms one 'box' or cycle. Repeat for four cycles.

- **Benefits:** Box breathing is effective in stress management, helping to clear the mind, relax the body, and improve focus.

Equal Breathing (Sama Vritti):

- **Technique:** Inhale through your nose for a count of four, then exhale through your nose for a count of four. Aim for equal length on both the inhale and exhale. As you get more practice, you can extend the count to six or eight.

- **Benefits:** Equal breathing can help reduce stress, increase focus, and promote a sense of balance and calm.

Guided Visualization with Breathing:

- **Technique:** Combine any of the above breathing techniques with guided visualization. As you engage in deep breathing, visualize a peaceful scene or experience. Imagine your stress and anxiety being released with each exhale.

- **Benefits:** Adding visualization can enhance the relaxation effect of breathing exercises, providing a mental escape and further reducing anxiety.

Implementing Breathing Techniques:

- **Practice Regularly:** Regular practice of these breathing exercises can enhance their effectiveness in managing anxiety. Encourage patients to practice daily, not just in moments of acute stress.

- **In-the-Moment Use:** Teach patients to use these techniques before and during medical appointments or any time they feel anxious.

- **Integration into Healthcare Settings:** Healthcare providers can support patients by creating a conducive environment for using these techniques, such as providing quiet spaces and encouraging their use before procedures.

Breathing techniques offer a simple yet profoundly effective way to manage the symptoms of White Coat Syndrome and other forms of anxiety. By incorporating these exercises into their coping toolkit, patients can gain immediate relief from stress, fostering a more positive healthcare experience.

4.2 Cognitive Behavioral Therapy (CBT) Approaches

Cognitive Behavioral Therapy (CBT) is a highly effective treatment for anxiety, including the specific anxieties related to White Coat Syndrome. CBT works by helping individuals identify and challenge negative thought patterns and beliefs that contribute to their anxiety and by teaching them practical skills to manage stressful situations. This subchapter explores various CBT approaches that can be particularly beneficial for patients experiencing White Coat Syndrome, aiming to provide them with strategies to cope with and ultimately reduce their anxiety in healthcare settings.

Identifying Cognitive Distortions:

- **Technique:** The first step in CBT is helping patients become aware of their automatic negative thoughts and the cognitive distortions that fuel their anxiety. Common distortions include catastrophizing (expecting the worst outcome), overgeneralization (viewing a single adverse event as a never-ending pattern of defeat), and mind reading (believing they know what others are thinking).

- **Application:** Patients learn to identify these distortions in their thoughts about medical visits or health outcomes and to challenge their validity.

Cognitive Restructuring:

- **Technique:** Cognitive restructuring involves teaching patients to challenge and reframe their negative thoughts into more balanced and accurate ones. For example, replacing the thought "The doctor will definitely find something wrong" with "The doctor is here to help me, and not all visits result in bad news."

- **Application:** Through practice, patients can begin to approach healthcare encounters with a more balanced and less fearful perspective.

Exposure Therapy:

- **Technique:** Exposure therapy, a component of CBT, involves gradual, controlled exposure to the source of one's fear to reduce the anxiety it causes. This is done in a safe and structured way, starting with less anxiety-inducing scenarios and gradually working up to more stressful ones.

- **Application:** For White Coat Syndrome, this could start with simply thinking about a medical visit, then progressing to sitting in a waiting room without having an appointment, and eventually going to medical appointments more calmly.

Relaxation and Stress Management Techniques:

- **Technique:** CBT also incorporates relaxation techniques, such as deep breathing, progressive muscle relaxation, and mindfulness meditation, to help manage the physiological symptoms of anxiety.

- **Application:** Patients are taught these techniques and encouraged to use them before and during medical visits to help control their anxiety levels.

Behavioral Experiments:

- **Technique:** Behavioral experiments are used to test the beliefs patients have about certain situations against reality. This might involve going to a medical appointment and observing that the outcomes are not as feared.

- **Application:** These experiments can help patients recalibrate their expectations and reduce anxiety over time.

Skill Development and Problem-Solving:

- **Technique:** CBT helps patients develop coping and problem-solving skills to deal with anxiety-provoking situations more effectively.

- **Application:** Patients learn to plan for and navigate healthcare encounters, such as preparing questions for their doctor or identifying specific fears and addressing them directly.

CBT is a collaborative process between the patient and therapist, focusing on achieving specific, measurable goals. For individuals with White Coat Syndrome, CBT provides a structured approach to understanding and managing their anxiety, offering tools that can be applied both within and outside healthcare settings. By working through these CBT approaches, patients can gain a greater sense of control over their anxiety, leading to more positive and less stressful healthcare experiences.

4.3 Long-Term Anxiety Management Strategies

For individuals experiencing White Coat Syndrome and related anxieties, developing long-term strategies for managing anxiety is crucial for improving health outcomes and overall quality of life. These strategies go beyond immediate coping mechanisms, focusing on building resilience, reducing vulnerability to stress, and fostering a more balanced emotional state over time. This subchapter outlines several critical approaches to long-term anxiety management, providing patients and healthcare providers with tools to address anxiety sustainably and effectively.

Lifestyle Modifications:

- **Regular Physical Activity:** Engaging in regular exercise has been shown to reduce symptoms of anxiety and depression significantly. Physical activity can help lower stress hormones and release endorphins, improving mood and reducing feelings of anxiety.

- **Healthy Diet:** A balanced diet can have a profound impact on mental health. Foods rich in omega-3 fatty acids, antioxidants, and vitamins can support brain health and reduce anxiety levels.

- **Adequate Sleep:** Poor sleep can exacerbate anxiety, while good sleep hygiene practices can help improve anxiety symptoms. Establishing a regular sleep schedule and creating a restful sleeping environment are critical components of managing stress in the long term.

Mindfulness and Meditation:

- **Practice Mindfulness:** Mindfulness involves paying attention to the present moment without judgment. Regular mindfulness practice can help individuals become more aware of their thoughts and feelings and less reactive to them, reducing overall anxiety.

- **Meditation:** Meditation techniques, such as guided imagery, progressive muscle relaxation, or mindfulness meditation, can be powerful tools for reducing stress and anxiety over time.

Building a Support System:

- **Social Support:** Strong social connections are essential for mental health. Encourage patients to cultivate relationships with friends, family, and support groups who can provide emotional support and understanding.

- **Professional Support:** For some, ongoing therapy with a psychologist or psychiatrist can be a critical component of managing long-term anxiety. This can include continued CBT, other forms of treatment, or medication management as needed.

Developing Coping Skills:

- **Stress Management Techniques:** Learning and regularly practicing stress management techniques, such as deep breathing exercises, yoga, or tai chi, can help individuals cope with anxiety triggers more effectively.

- **Cognitive Skills:** Continuing to practice cognitive restructuring and challenging irrational thoughts can help maintain the gains made through initial CBT or other therapies.

Self-Monitoring and Early Intervention:

- **Recognize Signs of Anxiety:** Encourage patients to become adept at recognizing the early signs of their anxiety, enabling them to implement coping strategies before symptoms escalate.

- **Proactive Management:** Encourage a proactive approach to managing stressors, including scheduling regular healthcare visits in a way that minimizes anxiety and addressing concerns directly with healthcare providers.

Education and Awareness:

- **Ongoing Education:** Staying informed about their health conditions and treatment options can empower patients and reduce feelings of helplessness and anxiety.

- **Awareness of Triggers:** Understanding and avoiding specific triggers, when possible, can help manage anxiety levels. This may include certain activities, caffeine, or stressful situations.

Implementing these long-term anxiety management strategies requires commitment and consistency but can lead to significant improvements in managing White Coat Syndrome and anxiety more broadly. By adopting a holistic approach that includes lifestyle changes, psychological strategies, and a supportive social network, individuals can build a foundation for enduring mental well-being and resilience.

4.4 Exercise: 10 MCQs with Answers at the End

This exercise aims to reinforce your understanding of long-term anxiety management strategies and specific approaches covered in Chapter 4: "Coping Mechanisms." Review these multiple-choice questions to test your grasp of the material and apply these concepts to managing White Coat Syndrome and general anxiety.

Questions:

1. Which lifestyle modification is known to reduce anxiety symptoms significantly?

    A. Increasing caffeine intake

    B. Regular physical activity

    C. Reduced sleep hours

    D. High-sugar diet

2. Mindfulness practices help manage anxiety by:

    A. Ignoring present-moment experiences

    B. Focusing on future events to prevent anxiety

    C. Paying attention to the present moment without judgment

    D. Distracting oneself with different activities

3. A balanced diet supporting mental health typically includes high amounts of:

    A. Saturated fats

    B. Fast food

    C. Omega-3 fatty acids

    D. Processed sugars

4. Which of the following is a benefit of adequate sleep in anxiety management?

   A. Increases stress hormone levels

   B. Exacerbates anxiety symptoms

   C. Improves mood and reduces feelings of anxiety

   D. None of the above

5. Social support in anxiety management can include:

   A. Isolating oneself from others

   B. Building relationships with friends, family, and support groups

   C. Avoiding all social interactions

   D. Sharing personal issues on social media platforms only

6. Cognitive Behavioral Therapy (CBT) approaches to long-term anxiety management DO NOT include:

   A. Engaging in regular exercise

   B. Identifying and challenging negative thought patterns

   C. Learning and practicing stress management techniques

   D. Avoiding all situations that may cause anxiety

7. Regular mindfulness and meditation practices are used in long-term anxiety management to:

   A. Increase the reactivity to stressful situations

   B. Reduce awareness of one's thoughts and feelings

   C. Help individuals become less reactive to their thoughts and feelings

   D. Focus exclusively on negative experiences

8. Developing coping skills for long-term anxiety management includes:

   A. Learning stress management techniques like yoga or tai chi

   B. Increasing dependency on medications only

   C. Ignoring signs of anxiety and stress

   D. Focusing on past events and regrets

9. The role of professional support in managing long-term anxiety may involve:

   A. Discontinuing any form of therapy

   B. Ongoing therapy with a psychologist or psychiatrist

   C. Relying solely on self-help books

   D. Avoiding discussions about anxiety with healthcare professionals

10. In long-term anxiety management, recognizing signs of anxiety early allows for:

   A. Implementation of coping strategies before symptoms escalate

   B. Complete avoidance of all healthcare visits

   C. Ignoring symptoms until they become severe

   D. Increased reliance on unhealthy coping mechanisms

Answers:

1. B. Regular physical activity

2. C. Paying attention to the present moment without judgment

3. C. Omega-3 fatty acids

4. C. Improves mood and reduces feelings of anxiety

5. B. Building relationships with friends, family, and support groups

6. D. Avoiding all situations that may cause anxiety

7. C. Help individuals become less reactive to their thoughts and feelings

8. A. Learning stress management techniques like yoga or tai chi

9. B. Ongoing therapy with a psychologist or psychiatrist

10. A. Implementation of coping strategies before symptoms escalate

These questions encapsulate key aspects of coping mechanisms and long-term anxiety management strategies discussed in Chapter 4, offering insights into how individuals can effectively manage White Coat Syndrome and general anxiety over time.

Chapter 5: The Power of Preparation

5.1 Educating Yourself Before Appointments

Empowering yourself with knowledge before medical appointments can significantly reduce anxiety and enhance your healthcare experience. Being informed about potential procedures, tests, or the nature of your consultation helps demystify the process, making the unknown less intimidating. This subchapter explores practical ways to educate yourself before appointments, focusing on strategies that can help individuals with White Coat Syndrome feel more in control and less anxious when facing medical encounters.

Research Your Condition:

- **Reputable Sources:** Seek information from reputable sources such as healthcare websites, medical journals, or patient education materials provided by your healthcare provider. Be cautious of misinformation from unverified online sources.

- **Understand Common Procedures:** Learn about standard procedures or tests you may undergo for your condition. Knowing what to expect can reduce fear of the unknown.

- **Symptom Tracking:** Keep a detailed record of your symptoms, including their frequency and severity. This can help your healthcare provider make a more accurate diagnosis and recommend appropriate treatment.

Prepare Questions in Advance:

- **List of Questions:** Write down any questions or concerns you have about your condition, treatment options, or the procedures you might undergo. Prioritize them in order of importance.

- **Specific Concerns:** If you have specific concerns about a procedure or medication, such as side effects or recovery time, make a note to discuss these with your healthcare provider.

Understand Your Treatment Options:

- **Treatment Research:** Educate yourself about the different treatment options available for your condition. This includes understanding the benefits, risks, and potential side effects.

- **Second Opinions:** Consider getting a second opinion if you are unsure about the recommended treatment plan. This can provide additional perspective and reassurance.

Utilize Patient Education Programs:

- **Hospital Resources:** Many hospitals and clinics offer patient education programs or classes that can provide valuable information about managing your condition, preparing for surgery, or understanding medications.

- **Online Resources:** Look for online resources, including webinars or interactive guides, offered by reputable healthcare organizations.

Engage with Support Groups:

- **Peer Support:** Connecting with others who have gone through similar health experiences can provide emotional support and practical advice. Support groups, either in-person or online, can offer insights into what to expect and how to prepare for medical appointments.

Communicate Openly with Your Healthcare Provider:

- **Share Your Research:** Discuss the information you've found with your healthcare provider. This can help clarify any misunderstandings and provide you with personalized advice based on your health status.

- **Express Concerns:** If your research has led to any concerns or questions, don't hesitate to bring them up. A good healthcare provider will welcome your engagement and provide clear, reassuring answers.

Benefits of Being Informed:

- **Reduced Anxiety:** Understanding your health condition and what to expect can significantly reduce anxiety related to the unknown.

- **Improved Outcomes:** Patients who are informed and engaged in their care often experience better health outcomes. Being prepared allows for a more collaborative relationship with your healthcare provider.

Educating yourself before medical appointments is a proactive step towards managing White Coat Syndrome and taking control of your healthcare journey. By arriving at appointments informed and prepared, you can reduce anxiety, improve communication with your healthcare provider, and make more informed decisions about your care.

5.2 The Checklist: What to Ask Your Doctor

Having a structured checklist of questions to ask your doctor can significantly improve the efficiency and effectiveness of your medical appointments, especially for those dealing with White Coat Syndrome. This approach ensures that all your concerns are addressed, helps you better understand your health condition, and fosters a more collaborative doctor-patient relationship. Here is a comprehensive checklist designed to guide you through the most critical aspects of your healthcare consultation.

Understanding Your Diagnosis:

1. **What is my diagnosis?**
2. **Can you explain my condition in simple terms?**
3. **Are there any common symptoms or signs I should watch for?**
4. **Is this condition temporary or chronic?**

Exploring Treatment Options:

5. **What treatment options are available for my condition?**
6. **What are the benefits and risks associated with these treatments?**
7. **Are there any lifestyle changes or non-medical interventions that can improve my condition?**
8. **What are the next steps if the initial treatment doesn't work?**

Understanding Tests and Procedures:

9. **What tests or procedures are you recommending?**

10. **How do these tests work, and what will they tell us?**

11. **Are there any preparations needed for the tests?**

12. **How and when will I receive the results?**

Managing Medications:

13. **Can you provide details on the prescribed medication(s)?**

14. **What are the possible side effects of this medication?**

15. **How should the medication be taken, and for how long?**

16. **Are there interactions with other medications or supplements I should be aware of?**

Considering Costs and Insurance:

17. **Will my insurance cover these treatments, tests, or medications?**

18. **Are there less expensive alternatives that are equally effective?**

19. **Can you provide any resources for financial assistance if needed?**

Planning Follow-Up Care:

20. **When should I schedule a follow-up appointment?**

21. **What symptoms should prompt me to contact your office sooner?**

22. **Who should I contact in case of an emergency or if I have urgent questions?**

General Health and Well-being:

23. **Are there any general lifestyle changes you recommend for improving my overall health?**

24. **How does my condition affect my daily life, and what adjustments should I make?**

25. **Can you recommend any resources for further information or support regarding my condition?**

This checklist serves as a starting point. Depending on your specific situation and condition, there might be additional questions that arise. Don't hesitate to add personalized queries that reflect your concerns and needs. Remember, the goal of your healthcare visit is not only to seek treatment but also to gain a deeper understanding of your health, ensuring you're an informed and active participant in your care.

5.3 Role-Playing and Scenario Planning

Role-playing and scenario planning are powerful techniques that can help individuals with White Coat Syndrome and other health-related anxieties prepare for medical appointments. These Strategies involve simulating healthcare interactions and planning for different outcomes, which can reduce stress by making the unknown more familiar and manageable. This subchapter discusses how to effectively use role-playing and scenario planning to prepare for medical visits, enhance communication with healthcare providers, and improve the overall healthcare experience.

Role-Playing for Medical Appointments:

- **Practice Conversations:** With the help of a friend, family member, or therapist, simulate the medical appointment by practicing conversations you might have with your doctor. Use your checklist of questions (as discussed in 5.2) to guide the discussion.

- **Simulate Scenarios:** Prepare for various responses from the healthcare provider, including best-case and worst-case scenarios. Practicing how to respond to different types of news can help reduce anxiety when faced with the actual situation.

- **Non-Verbal Communication:** Pay attention to non-verbal cues during the role-play. Practice maintaining eye contact, controlling nervous habits, and using body language that conveys confidence and openness.

Scenario Planning:

- **Outline Possible Outcomes:** Before your appointment, think about the potential outcomes of your visit. This might include receiving a diagnosis, being prescribed medication, needing further tests, or being referred to a specialist.

- **Develop a Plan for Each Outcome:** For each possible scenario, outline a plan of action. This might involve researching treatment options, scheduling follow-up appointments, or discussing findings with family members.

- **Mental Preparation:** Mentally walk through each scenario, imagining how you would react and what steps you would take. Visualize yourself handling the situation calmly and effectively.

Benefits of Role-Playing and Scenario Planning:

- **Reduced Anxiety:** By familiarizing yourself with the healthcare environment and potential conversations, you can reduce the fear of the unknown that often fuels anxiety.

- **Improved Communication Skills:** Practicing discussions with healthcare providers can improve your ability to ask questions clearly and express your concerns effectively.

- **Enhanced Coping Strategies:** Preparing for different outcomes helps develop resilience and flexibility, enabling you to cope more effectively with any news or recommendations received during the appointment.

Incorporating Mindfulness and Relaxation:

- **Integrate Breathing Techniques:** Use deep breathing exercises before and during role-playing or scenario planning to manage anxiety and maintain focus.

- **Mindfulness:** Practice mindfulness to stay present during the exercises, acknowledging any anxious thoughts or feelings without judgment and gently redirecting your attention back to the task at hand.

Seeking Professional Guidance:

- **Guidance from Therapists:** If available, consider working with a therapist who can guide you through role-playing and scenario planning exercises, providing professional feedback and coping strategies.

Role-playing and scenario planning are proactive steps towards demystifying medical appointments and building confidence in navigating the healthcare system. By preparing mentally and emotionally for various outcomes, individuals with White Coat Syndrome can approach medical visits with greater calmness and assurance, leading to more positive healthcare experiences.

5.4 Exercise: 10 MCQs with Answers at the End

This exercise is designed to test your understanding of the concepts covered in Chapter 5: "The Power of Preparation," focusing on educating yourself before appointments, what to ask your doctor, role-playing, and scenario planning, and their importance in managing White Coat Syndrome and reducing healthcare-related anxiety.

Questions:

1. Educating yourself before a medical appointment can:

    A. Increase anxiety due to overthinking.

    B. Lead to self-diagnosis and misinterpretation.

    C. Reduce anxiety by making the unknown more familiar.

    D. Discourage communication with healthcare providers.

2. When preparing questions to ask your doctor, it's essential to:

    A. Ask about the latest medical rumors.

    B. Focus only on questions with simple yes or no answers.

    C. Prioritize your questions in order of importance.

    D. Avoid asking about side effects to avoid seeming distrustful.

3. Role-playing before a medical appointment can help with:

   A. Memorizing a script to avoid genuine conversation.

   B. Practicing conversations and improving communication skills.

   C. Increasing dependence on others for healthcare decisions.

   D. Avoiding important but uncomfortable topics.

4. Scenario planning for medical appointments allows you to:

   A. eliminate the possibility of receiving unexpected news.

   B. Prepare for different outcomes and develop plans of action.

   C. Focus only on worst-case scenarios to brace yourself for bad news.

   D. Ignore the need for follow-up appointments or further testing.

5. A key benefit of educating yourself about your condition is:

   A. The ability to challenge the doctor's expertise.

   B. Reduced reliance on healthcare professionals for information.

   C. Improved ability to make informed decisions about your care.

   D. Encouragement to seek alternative and unverified treatments.

6. The checklist of questions to ask your doctor should NOT include:

   A. Requests for clarification on medical jargon.

   B. Personal medical advice found on online forums.

   C. Information on potential side effects of prescribed medications.

   D. Details about how to prepare for or recover from procedures.

7. Effective role-playing involves:

   A. Only rehearsing positive outcomes to stay optimistic.

   B. Simulating various scenarios, including receiving different types of news.

   C. Practicing aggressive negotiation tactics for treatment costs.

   D. Using medical jargon to impress the healthcare provider.

8. In scenario planning, it's essential to:

   A. Only consider the most likely outcome to avoid confusion.

   B. Develop a plan of action for each possible outcome.

   C. Assume all scenarios will lead to negative consequences.

   D. Avoid discussing your plans with your healthcare provider.

9. One reason to prioritize your questions for the doctor is to:

   A. Minimize the time spent on the appointment.

   B. Ensure the most important concerns are addressed first.

   C. Keep the conversation limited to non-serious issues.

   D. Impress the doctor with your efficiency.

10. Practicing mindfulness and relaxation techniques before role-playing:

   A. Is unnecessary if you are already familiar with the medical environment.

   B. Can increase anxiety by focusing too much on the appointment.

   C. Helps manage anxiety and maintain focus during the exercise.

   D. Should only be done in the presence of a healthcare professional.

Answers:

1. C. Reduce anxiety by making the unknown more familiar.

2. C. Prioritize your questions in order of importance.

3. B. Practicing conversations and improving communication skills.

4. B. Prepare for different outcomes and develop plans of action.

5. C. Improved ability to make informed decisions about your care.

6. B. Personal medical advice found on online forums.

7. B. Simulating various scenarios, including receiving different types of news.

8. B. Develop a plan of action for each possible outcome.

9. B. Ensure the most important concerns are addressed first.

10. C. Helps manage anxiety and maintain focus during the exercise.

These questions highlight the importance of preparation and informed participation in healthcare settings, especially for individuals experiencing White Coat Syndrome or healthcare-related anxiety.

Chapter 6: Technological Aids and Mobile Apps

6.1 Apps for Meditation and Relaxation

In the digital age, technological aids, particularly mobile apps, have become invaluable tools for managing anxiety, including the stresses associated with White Coat Syndrome. Apps designed for meditation and relaxation can offer immediate, accessible support to individuals seeking to manage their anxiety levels, providing a range of functionalities from guided meditations to stress-reduction exercises. This subchapter explores some of the most effective apps available for meditation and relaxation, highlighting how they can be integrated into daily routines to help manage healthcare-related anxieties.

Headspace:

- **Overview:** Headspace is a widely recognized meditation app that offers guided meditations, mindfulness practices, and breathing exercises. It's designed to help users reduce stress, improve sleep, and increase overall well-being.

- **Features:** Users can access sessions of varying lengths tailored to specific needs, such as anxiety reduction, focus improvement, or relaxation to aid sleep.

- **Benefits:** Regular use of Headspace can help individuals develop a consistent meditation practice, which can be particularly beneficial before medical appointments or in managing long-term anxiety.

Calm:

- **Overview:** Calm is another popular app that provides guided meditations, sleep stories, breathing programs, and relaxing music. It is designed to help lower stress, alleviate anxiety, and promote better sleep.

- **Features:** Includes a wide range of meditation topics, such as calming anxiety, managing stress, and focusing. Calm also offers nature sounds and scenes to enhance relaxation.

- **Benefits:** Calm's varied content can suit different preferences and needs, making it a versatile tool for individuals looking to find peace and reduce anxiety in various situations, including before healthcare visits.

Insight Timer:

- **Overview:** Insight Timer boasts an extensive library of free meditations contributed by mindfulness experts, therapists, and teachers from around the world. It covers a vast array of topics, including anxiety management, stress reduction, and sleep improvement.

- **Features:** Offers guided meditations, music tracks, and ambient sounds. Users can also track their meditation progress and connect with a global meditation community.

- **Benefits:** The extensive library allows users to explore different meditation styles and find the ones that best suit their anxiety management needs.

10% Happier:

- **Overview:** 10% Happier caters to skeptics and beginners by offering a practical approach to meditation and mindfulness. It includes guided meditations, videos, and talks designed to make meditation accessible and relatable.

- **Features:** Provides courses on various themes, including stress reduction, happiness, and resilience, with a focus on practical techniques.

- **Benefits:** The app's straightforward approach can help individuals new to meditation start a practice that supports anxiety management, including preparing for medical appointments.

Breathe:

- **Overview:** Breathe is a comprehensive app that guides users through various aspects of meditation, including techniques to overcome insomnia, anxiety, and stress.

- **Features:** Includes guided meditations, hypnotherapy sessions, inspirational talks, and masterclasses. Breethe also offers personalized meditation recommendations.

- **Benefits:** Breethe's wide range of content addresses not just immediate relaxation needs but also offers tools for long-term stress and anxiety management.

Integrating Meditation Apps into Your Routine:

- **Daily Practice:** Incorporate meditation and relaxation exercises into your daily routine to build resilience against anxiety over time.

- **Pre-Appointment Use:** Use meditation or relaxation apps before medical appointments to reduce anxiety and arrive in a calmer state.

- **Customization:** Explore different apps and features to find what best suits your preferences and needs, customizing your meditation practice to your lifestyle.

Meditation and relaxation apps offer a practical and accessible way to manage anxiety, providing tools that can be seamlessly integrated into daily life. For individuals experiencing White Coat Syndrome, these apps can be beneficial in preparing for medical encounters, fostering a sense of calm and control.

6.2 Tracking Your Health Anxiety Trends

In managing health-related anxiety, especially conditions like White Coat Syndrome, tracking and understanding the patterns and triggers of your anxiety can be incredibly beneficial. With the advent of technology, numerous apps and digital tools have been developed to help individuals monitor their anxiety levels, identify specific triggers, and observe trends over time. This subchapter focuses on how leveraging these technological aids can empower individuals to gain insights into their health anxiety trends, enabling more targeted and effective management strategies.

Benefits of Tracking Health Anxiety Trends:

- **Increased Self-Awareness:** Regular tracking helps you become more aware of the situations, times, and conditions that elevate your anxiety levels. This awareness is the first step in developing coping strategies.

- **Data-Driven Insights:** Over time, the data collected can reveal patterns in your anxiety levels, offering insights into how various factors like sleep, diet, and exercise influence your anxiety.

- **Personalized Management Plans:** Understanding your anxiety trends allows you to tailor your anxiety management strategies more effectively, focusing on what works best for you.

Technological Aids for Tracking Anxiety:

Mood Tracking Apps:

- Apps like **Moodfit**, **Daylio**, and **Sanvello** allow users to record their mood and anxiety levels daily. Many of these apps offer the functionality to note specific events, activities, or triggers associated with fluctuations in anxiety levels, enabling users to identify patterns over time.

Health and Wellness Apps:

- Comprehensive health apps that track various aspects of physical health, such as **MyFitnessPal** and **Apple Health**, can also be used to correlate anxiety levels with physical activity, sleep patterns, and dietary habits, providing a holistic view of how lifestyle factors impact anxiety.

Wearable Technology:

- Devices like **Fitbit**, **Apple Watch**, and **Garmin** can monitor physiological indicators of stress and anxiety, such as heart rate variability. By correlating this data with self-reported mood and anxiety levels, individuals can gain a deeper understanding of their physical responses to stress.

Journaling Apps:

- Digital journaling apps like **Journey** and **Reflectly** offer a platform for reflective writing, which can be used to document thoughts, feelings, and circumstances surrounding episodes of anxiety, facilitating a deeper exploration of triggers and coping mechanisms.

Implementing Tracking into Daily Life:

1. **Consistency:** For tracking to be effective, it's essential to record your anxiety levels and related factors consistently, aiming for daily entries.

2. **Holistic Tracking:** Consider tracking not just your anxiety levels but also related lifestyle factors such as sleep, exercise, caffeine intake, and significant life events.

3. **Review and Reflect:** Regularly review the data and notes you've collected to identify any trends or patterns. Reflect on what changes might help manage your anxiety more effectively.

4. **Share with Healthcare Providers:** Sharing your tracking data with healthcare providers can offer valuable insights during consultations, enabling more personalized care and targeted anxiety management strategies.

Utilizing Technology for Self-Empowerment:

Embracing technology to track health anxiety trends empowers individuals to take an active role in managing their anxiety. By providing concrete data and insights, technological aids support the development of personalized and effective anxiety management plans. For those dealing with White Coat Syndrome, this proactive approach can significantly improve the experience of medical appointments and overall well-being.

6.3 Virtual Reality Exposure Therapy

Virtual Reality Exposure Therapy (VRET) represents a cutting-edge intersection of technology and mental health treatment, offering a novel approach to managing conditions like White Coat Syndrome. By simulating real-world environments and scenarios that trigger anxiety, VRET allows individuals to confront and gradually desensitize their fears in a controlled, safe setting. This subchapter delves into the principles, benefits, and applications of VRET in treating health-related anxieties, highlighting its potential to transform the way individuals prepare for and experience medical environments.

Principles of VRET:

- **Controlled Exposure:** VRET utilizes virtual reality technology to create immersive simulations of anxiety-provoking scenarios, such as visiting a doctor's office or undergoing medical procedures. This controlled exposure enables individuals to face their fears without real-world consequences.

- **Graduated Challenges:** The therapy can be tailored to present challenges in a graduated manner, starting from less anxiety-inducing scenarios and progressively moving towards more challenging situations, allowing for gradual desensitization.

- **Real-Time Feedback:** Participants receive immediate feedback on their reactions and can practice coping strategies within the virtual environment, enhancing their ability to manage anxiety in real situations.

Benefits of VRET:

- **Safety and Privacy:** VRET provides a safe and private environment for individuals to confront their fears, reducing the potential for embarrassment or discomfort that might occur in real-world settings.

- **Repeatability:** Scenarios can be repeated as often as necessary, providing ample opportunity for practice and mastery of anxiety management techniques.

- **Customization:** Virtual environments and scenarios can be customized to match each individual's specific fears and triggers, making the therapy highly personalized and effective.

Applications in Managing White Coat Syndrome:

- **Simulating Medical Visits:** VRET can simulate various aspects of medical visits, from waiting rooms to consultations and procedures, helping individuals acclimate to these environments and reduce anticipatory anxiety.

- **Practicing Coping Strategies:** Within the virtual environment, individuals can practice breathing exercises, mindfulness, and other coping strategies to manage their anxiety, reinforcing these skills for use in actual medical settings.

- **Enhancing Patient Education:** VRET can also be used as an educational tool, providing interactive experiences that explain medical procedures or treatments, thereby reducing fear of the unknown.

Implementing VRET:

- **Access Through Professionals:** Access to VRET is typically provided through mental health professionals who specialize in anxiety disorders and are trained in VRET protocols. They can guide individuals through the process, ensuring the therapy is conducted safely and effectively.

- **Integration with Traditional Therapy:** VRET is often most effective when integrated with traditional therapy approaches, such as cognitive-behavioral therapy (CBT), providing a comprehensive treatment plan for managing anxiety.

Future Directions:

The ongoing development of VRET technology promises to enhance its accessibility and effectiveness. Future iterations may include more realistic simulations, interactive elements that allow for even greater customization, and integration with biofeedback to monitor physiological responses in real time.

Conclusion:

Virtual Reality Exposure Therapy offers a promising avenue for individuals struggling with White Coat Syndrome and other forms of health-related anxiety. By providing a realistic yet controlled environment to confront and manage fears, VRET represents a significant advance in anxiety treatment, empowering individuals to take control of their anxiety in a novel and engaging way.

6.4 Exercise: 10 MCQs with Answers at the End

Test your understanding of the technological aids and mobile apps designed to assist with managing health-related anxiety, including meditation and relaxation apps, tracking health anxiety trends, and the innovative use of Virtual Reality Exposure Therapy (VRET).

Questions:

1. What is the primary purpose of meditation and relaxation apps like Headspace and Calm?

   A. To track physical activity

   B. To provide guided meditations for stress reduction

   C. To monitor dietary intake

   D. To increase productivity

2. How can mood-tracking apps benefit individuals with health-related anxiety?

   A. By encouraging social media use

   B. By identifying patterns and triggers of anxiety

   C. By increasing screen time

   D. By promoting a sedentary lifestyle

3. What feature is common among health and wellness apps like MyFitnessPal and Apple Health?

   A. Virtual reality experiences

   B. Correlating lifestyle factors with anxiety levels

   C. Online Gaming

   D. Live streaming workouts

4. Virtual Reality Exposure Therapy (VRET) is primarily used to:

   A. Enhance video gaming skills

   B. Simulate environments for anxiety desensitization

   C. Track heart rate and physical activity

   D. Improve virtual social skills

5. The process of gradually increasing the difficulty of scenarios in VRET is known as:

   A. Leveling up

   B. Graduated challenges

   C. Customization

   D. Real-time feedback

6. Which of the following is NOT a direct benefit of using meditation apps?

   A. Immediate relief from stress

   B. Customized diet plans

   C. Improved sleep quality

   D. Enhanced focus and mindfulness

7. Tracking health anxiety trends can help in:

   A. Decreasing awareness of one's condition

   B. Developing targeted management strategies

C. Ignoring underlying health issues

D. Focusing solely on adverse outcomes

8. Wearable technology like Fitbit and Apple Watch can be used to:

   A. Play virtual reality games

   B. Monitor physiological indicators of stress

   C. Replace professional medical advice

   D. Diagnose health conditions

9. Role-playing and scenario planning before medical appointments can improve:

   A. Dependency on technology

   B. Communication skills and preparedness

   C. Interest in medical careers

   D. Virtual social connections

10. an essential feature of VRET in managing White Coat Syndrome is:

    A. Providing real-time weather updates

    B. Simulating medical environments for desensitization

    C. Tracking daily step count

    D. Offering virtual travel experiences

Answers:

1. B. To provide guided meditations for stress reduction
2. B. By identifying patterns and triggers of anxiety
3. B. Correlating lifestyle factors with anxiety levels
4. B. Simulate environments for anxiety desensitization
5. B. Graduated challenges
6. B. Customized diet plans
7. B. Developing targeted management strategies
8. B. Monitor physiological indicators of stress
9. B. Communication skills and preparedness
10. B. Simulating medical environments for desensitization

These questions are designed to reinforce your knowledge of how technology, including apps and VRET, can be leveraged to manage health-related anxiety effectively, providing insights into their functionalities and benefits.

Chapter 7: Lifestyle Adjustments

7.1 Diet and Exercise

Lifestyle adjustments, particularly in the realms of diet and exercise, play a crucial role in managing health-related anxieties such as White Coat Syndrome. A balanced diet and regular physical activity can significantly impact mental health, helping to reduce symptoms of anxiety and improve overall well-being. This subchapter explores the relationship between diet, exercise, and anxiety management, offering guidance on how to integrate these elements into your lifestyle for better health outcomes.

The Impact of Diet on Anxiety:

- **Nutrient-Rich Foods:** Consuming a diet rich in vitamins, minerals, and antioxidants can support brain health and reduce anxiety. Foods high in omega-3 fatty acids (such as salmon and flaxseeds), magnesium (such as leafy greens and nuts), and vitamins B and D are particularly beneficial.

- **Avoiding Stimulants:** Caffeine and sugar can exacerbate anxiety symptoms for some individuals. Monitoring and possibly reducing intake of these substances can help in managing anxiety levels.

- **Hydration:** Proper hydration is essential for optimal brain function and mood regulation. Dehydration can cause or worsen feelings of anxiety and stress.

Exercise as a Tool for Anxiety Management:

- **Regular Physical Activity:** Engaging in regular exercise, such as walking, running, cycling, or yoga, can help lower anxiety levels by releasing endorphins, natural mood elevators, and stress relievers.

- **Exercise and Stress Response:** Regular physical activity can reduce the body's stress hormones, such as adrenaline and cortisol, over time. It also improves sleep, which can be negatively affected by anxiety.

- **Finding the Right Balance:** It's important to find a type of exercise that you enjoy and can stick with. Overexercising can lead to increased stress, so balance is critical.

Integrating Diet and Exercise into Your Routine:

- **Start Small:** Make small, manageable changes to your diet and exercise routine. Gradually incorporating healthier food choices and regular physical activity can make these adjustments more sustainable.

- **Mindful Eating:** Pay attention to how your body feels after eating certain foods. Mindful eating can help you identify foods that may affect your anxiety levels.

- **Set Realistic Goals:** Set achievable goals for your diet and exercise plan. Celebrate small victories to stay motivated.

- **Seek Professional Advice:** Consider consulting with a nutritionist or personal trainer to develop a plan tailored to your needs, especially if you have specific health conditions or dietary restrictions.

The Synergistic Effect of Diet and Exercise:

Combining a healthy diet with regular exercise can have a synergistic effect on reducing anxiety. Together, they can improve physical health, enhance mental clarity, and provide a sense of well-being, making them powerful tools in managing White Coat Syndrome and other forms of health-related anxiety.

Conclusion:

Adopting lifestyle adjustments in diet and exercise is a proactive approach to managing anxiety. By nurturing your body with the proper nutrients and keeping it active, you can create a strong foundation for mental health and resilience against stressors, including those related to healthcare experiences.

7.2 Sleep Hygiene and Its Impact on Anxiety

Sleep hygiene refers to the practices and habits that are conducive to sleeping well on a regular basis. Good sleep hygiene is crucial for mental health, as poor sleep can significantly exacerbate anxiety, including the symptoms of White Coat Syndrome. This subchapter explores the relationship between sleep hygiene and anxiety, offering strategies to improve sleep quality and thereby reduce anxiety levels.

The Connection Between Sleep and Anxiety:

- **Bidirectional Relationship:** The relationship between sleep and anxiety is bidirectional. Anxiety can lead to sleep disturbances, while poor sleep can increase the likelihood of experiencing anxiety.

- **Impact on Stress Hormones:** Lack of sleep can elevate cortisol levels, the body's primary stress hormone, thereby increasing feelings of anxiety and making it harder to calm down.

- **REM Sleep and Emotional Regulation:** Rapid Eye Movement (REM) sleep, a phase of deep sleep associated with dreaming, is essential for emotional regulation. Disruptions in REM sleep can impair the ability to process emotional experiences, contributing to heightened anxiety.

Improving Sleep Hygiene:

- **Consistent Sleep Schedule:** Going to bed and waking up at the same time every day, including weekends, can help regulate your body's internal clock and improve the quality of your sleep.

- **Create a Restful Environment:** Ensure your sleeping environment is conducive to rest. This means a comfortable mattress and pillows, a cool room temperature, and minimal noise and light.

- **Limit Screen Time Before Bed:** Exposure to the blue light emitted by screens can interfere with your ability to fall asleep. Try to limit the use of electronic devices for at least an hour before bedtime.

- **Relaxation Techniques:** Incorporating relaxation techniques into your bedtime routine, such as reading, meditation, or deep breathing exercises, can help prepare your mind and body for sleep.

- **Avoid Stimulants:** Avoid consuming caffeine and nicotine close to bedtime, as they can interfere with your ability to fall asleep. Also, be mindful of alcohol consumption, as it can disrupt sleep later in the night.

Exercise and Diet Impact on Sleep:

- **Physical Activity:** Regular physical activity can help you fall asleep faster and enjoy deeper sleep. However, try to avoid vigorous exercise close to bedtime, as it may have the opposite effect.

- **Diet:** Eating a heavy meal right before bed can lead to discomfort and indigestion, making it harder to sleep. Try to eat dinner at least a few hours before bedtime and opt for light, easily digestible snacks if you're hungry later.

When to Seek Professional Help:

- **Persistent Sleep Issues:** If you've tried improving your sleep hygiene but still struggle with sleep disturbances or insomnia, it may be time to seek professional help. A healthcare provider can assess your situation and may recommend further interventions, such as cognitive-behavioral therapy for insomnia (CBT-I) or medication.

- **Connection to Anxiety Disorders:** For some individuals, sleep issues are closely tied to underlying anxiety disorders. Addressing the anxiety directly through therapy or medication can also improve sleep quality.

Conclusion:

Good sleep hygiene is an essential component of managing anxiety. By fostering habits that promote restful sleep, individuals can reduce the impact of stress on their lives, including the specific anxieties associated with medical visits and White Coat Syndrome. Prioritizing sleep is not just about physical rest; it's about giving your brain the time it needs to process emotions, reduce stress, and recharge for the day ahead.

7.3 The Role of Social Support

Social support plays a critical role in managing anxiety, including the apprehensions associated with White Coat Syndrome. It encompasses the emotional, informational, and practical assistance received from family, friends, healthcare professionals, and support groups. This subchapter explores how social support can influence anxiety levels and offers strategies for cultivating a supportive network to navigate health-related challenges more effectively.

Impact of Social Support on Anxiety:

- **Emotional Buffer:** Social support acts as an emotional buffer against stress and anxiety. Knowing you have people who care about and support you can significantly reduce feelings of isolation and helplessness.

- **Information Sharing:** Friends and family can provide valuable information and insights, including personal experiences with similar health issues, which can demystify medical procedures and reduce anxiety.

- **Practical Help:** Support networks can offer practical assistance, such as accompanying you to medical appointments, which can be exceptionally comforting if you're nervous about visits or procedures.

Cultivating Social Support:

- **Communicate Openly:** Be open about your feelings and fears regarding your health and medical appointments. People often want to help but may not know how unless you communicate your needs.

- **Engage with Support Groups:** Support groups, whether in-person or online, connect you with individuals facing similar health challenges. These groups can provide a sense of community, shared understanding, and valuable coping strategies.

- **Leverage Technology:** Social media and other digital platforms can help you maintain connections with your support network, share experiences, and access emotional support anytime.

- **Seek Professional Support:** Therapists and counselors can offer professional emotional support and teach coping mechanisms for managing anxiety. They can also help you build strategies for enhancing your social support network.

Strengthening Relationships:

- **Quality Over Quantity:** Focus on strengthening quality relationships with a few key people rather than trying to maintain a vast network of superficial connections.

- **Reciprocity:** Supportive relationships are reciprocal. Be ready to offer support to others in your network when they need it, fostering a mutual support system.

- **Set Boundaries:** Healthy relationships require boundaries. Communicate your needs clearly and respectfully, and be mindful of the boundaries of others in your support network.

The Role of Healthcare Professionals:

- **Part of Your Support Network:** View healthcare professionals as part of your support network. Building a trusting relationship with your doctor, nurse, or therapist can provide reassurance and reduce anxiety related to medical care.

- **Ask for Referrals:** If you're struggling to find support, ask healthcare professionals for referrals to support groups, counseling services, or other resources.

The Importance of Social Support in Health Outcomes:

Research has consistently shown that strong social support is linked to better mental and physical health outcomes. For individuals dealing with White Coat Syndrome or other forms of health-related anxiety, social support can:

- Improve adherence to treatment plans.

- Increase satisfaction with healthcare experiences.

- Enhance resilience against stress.

Conclusion:

Social support is a vital component of managing anxiety and navigating health-related challenges. By actively cultivating and maintaining supportive relationships, individuals can enhance their ability to cope with White Coat Syndrome and improve their overall well-being. Encouraging open communication, engaging with support groups, and leveraging the support of healthcare professionals are critical strategies for building a robust support network.

7.4 Exercise: 10 MCQs with Answers at the End

Test your knowledge of the lifestyle adjustments crucial for managing health-related anxiety, focusing on diet and exercise, sleep hygiene, the importance of social support, and their collective impact on well-being.

Questions:

1. Which of the following has been shown to reduce anxiety symptoms: A diet rich in:

   A. Saturated fats

   B. Omega-3 fatty acids

C. Processed sugars

D. Artificial additives

2. Regular physical activity benefits mental health by:

    A. Increasing stress levels

    B. Releasing endorphins that act as natural mood lifters

    C. Promoting sedentary behavior

    D. Reducing the need for sleep

3. Good sleep hygiene practices include:

    A. Using electronic devices right before bed

    B. Going to bed and waking up at the same time daily

    C. Consuming large meals immediately before bedtime

    D. Keeping the bedroom warm and well-lit

4. Social support can help manage anxiety by:

    A. Encouraging isolation

    B. Providing emotional and practical assistance

    C. Promoting dependency on others

    D. Limiting information sharing

5. The bidirectional relationship between sleep and anxiety means:

   A. Sleep quality and anxiety levels do not affect each other

   B. Improving sleep can help reduce anxiety and vice versa

   C. Only anxiety influences sleep quality

   D. Only sleep quality can affect anxiety levels

6. One effective way to manage dietary intake to reduce anxiety is to:

   A. Increase caffeine consumption

   B. Avoid foods high in omega-3 fatty acids

   C. Monitor and possibly reduce caffeine and sugar intake

   D. Focus on a high-sugar diet

7. Which is NOT a benefit of engaging in regular exercise for anxiety management?

   A. Improved focus and clarity

   B. Enhanced physical fitness only, with no mental health benefits

   C. Lowered levels of stress hormones

   D. Better quality of sleep

8. The primary purpose of joining support groups for managing health-related anxiety is to:

   A. Avoid dealing with anxiety alone

   B. Share experiences and coping strategies

   C. Promote a sense of competition

   D. Limit social interactions to digital platforms

9. In the context of sleep hygiene, REM sleep is essential because:

   A. It is when the body requires the most caffeine

   B. It doesn't impact mental or emotional health

   C. It plays a crucial role in emotional regulation

   D. It decreases the body's need for deep sleep

10. Strengthening quality relationships to enhance social support involves:

   A. Maintaining a vast network of superficial connections

   B. Reciprocity and mutual support

   C. Encouraging dependency on others

   D. Isolating oneself from others to manage anxiety independently

Answers:

1. B. Omega-3 fatty acids

2. B. Releasing endorphins that act as natural mood lifters

3. B. Going to bed and waking up at the same time daily

4. B. Providing emotional and practical assistance

5. B. Improving sleep can help reduce anxiety and vice versa

6. C. Monitor and possibly reduce caffeine and sugar intake

7. B. Enhanced physical fitness only, with no mental health benefits

8. B. Share experiences and coping strategies

9. C. It plays a crucial role in emotional regulation

10. B. Reciprocity and mutual support

These questions are designed to enhance your understanding of how diet, exercise, sleep hygiene, and social support play critical roles in managing health-related anxiety, including White Coat Syndrome, and improving overall mental health and well-being.

Chapter 8: Understanding the Healthcare System

8.1 Navigating Healthcare Settings

Navigating healthcare settings can be daunting, especially for individuals experiencing White Coat Syndrome or other forms of health-related anxiety. Understanding how to navigate these environments effectively is crucial for receiving quality care and minimizing stress. This subchapter provides insights and strategies for successfully navigating healthcare settings, enhancing patient empowerment, and reducing anxiety associated with medical visits.

Familiarize Yourself with the Healthcare System:

- **Research Healthcare Providers:** Take the time to research and choose healthcare providers who are known for their patient-centered care approach. Look for providers who communicate clearly, show empathy, and are willing to address your concerns.

- **Understand Your Health Insurance:** Familiarize yourself with your health insurance plan's coverage, including which services are covered, your deductibles, copayments, and the network of providers available to you.

Preparing for Healthcare Visits:

- **Gather Necessary Documentation:** Prepare any necessary documentation in advance, such as identification, insurance cards, medical records, and a list of current medications. Having these documents ready can help reduce stress on the day of your visit.

- **Write Down Your Health Concerns:** Before your appointment, write down any symptoms, concerns, or questions you have. This can help ensure you cover all essential points during your visit.

- **Bring a Support Person:** If possible, bring a friend or family member with you to your appointments. Having someone there for emotional support can make the experience less intimidating.

Effective Communication with Healthcare Providers:

- **Be Open and Honest:** Communicate openly with your healthcare provider about your symptoms, concerns, and any anxiety you feel about medical visits or procedures.

- **Ask Questions:** Don't hesitate to ask questions or request further explanations if something is unclear. Understanding your health condition and treatment options is critical to reducing anxiety.

- **Provide Feedback:** Share your feelings about the care you're receiving. If something makes you uncomfortable, let your healthcare provider know.

Utilizing Patient Resources:

- **Patient Advocacy Services:** Many healthcare facilities offer patient advocacy services to help navigate the system, understand patient rights, and communicate with healthcare providers.

- **Educational Materials:** Take advantage of any educational materials or resources offered by your healthcare provider or facility to learn more about your condition and treatment options.

Dealing with Healthcare Bureaucracy:

- **Keep Records:** Maintain your records of medical visits, treatments, and test results. This can be helpful for future appointments or if you need to see a specialist.

- **Patient Portals:** Many healthcare providers offer online patient portals where you can access your medical records, schedule appointments, and communicate with your healthcare team. Utilizing these tools can streamline the management of your healthcare.

Conclusion:

Navigating healthcare settings with confidence is a vital skill for managing health-related anxiety and ensuring positive healthcare experiences. By preparing in advance, communicating effectively with healthcare providers, and utilizing available resources, patients can mitigate the stress associated with medical visits and become active participants in their healthcare journey. Empowerment and education are vital to navigating healthcare settings successfully and enhancing overall satisfaction with the healthcare system.

8.2 Patient Rights and Advocacy

Understanding patient rights and the role of advocacy within healthcare is essential for navigating the healthcare system, particularly for individuals who experience health-related anxieties such as White Coat Syndrome. Patient rights are designed to protect individuals in healthcare settings, ensuring they receive respectful, confidential, and competent care. Advocacy, whether self-advocacy or through the support of others, empowers patients to make informed decisions about their health and to seek the best possible care. This subchapter delves into the core aspects of patient rights and the significance of advocacy in enhancing healthcare experiences.

Understanding Patient Rights:

- **Right to Informed Consent:** Patients have the right to receive clear, understandable information about their diagnosis, treatment options, and potential risks associated with each option. Informed consent ensures that patients are actively involved in decisions about their care.

- **Right to Privacy and Confidentiality:** Health information is personal and sensitive. Patients have the right to expect that all communications and records pertaining to their care are treated with the utmost confidentiality.

- **Right to Respect and Dignity:** Regardless of race, gender, age, or condition, patients deserve to be treated with respect and dignity by all healthcare providers.

- **Right to Second Opinion:** Patients have the right to seek a second opinion from another healthcare provider if they wish to confirm a diagnosis or explore alternative treatment options.

The Importance of Advocacy:

- **Self-Advocacy:** Empowering oneself with knowledge about one's condition and rights as a patient is a form of self-advocacy. Being able to articulate your needs and concerns to healthcare providers is crucial for receiving appropriate care.

- **Professional Advocates:** Patient advocates or navigators can assist individuals in understanding their rights, making informed decisions, and communicating effectively with healthcare professionals. They can also help navigate the complexities of the healthcare system, including insurance issues and accessing care.

- **Support Networks:** Friends, family members, or caregivers can also serve as advocates, providing emotional support, assisting with decision-making, and helping to communicate with healthcare providers.

Strategies for Effective Advocacy:

- **Educate Yourself:** Learn as much as you can about your condition, treatment options, and the healthcare system. Knowledge is power when it comes to advocating for your health.

- **Communicate Clearly:** Develop the skills to communicate effectively with your healthcare providers. Be clear about your symptoms, concerns, and preferences.

- **Document Everything:** Keep detailed records of your medical history, treatments, medications, and interactions with healthcare providers. This documentation can be invaluable in managing your care and advocating for your needs.

- **Know Your Rights:** Familiarize yourself with patient rights in your country or region, as these can vary. Knowing your rights can help you advocate more effectively for the care you deserve.

Conclusion:

Understanding and exercising patient rights, coupled with effective advocacy, are fundamental to navigating the healthcare system and ensuring positive healthcare outcomes. For those dealing with White Coat Syndrome or other health-related anxieties, becoming an informed and proactive participant in your healthcare can alleviate some of the stress and uncertainty associated with medical visits. Whether through self-advocacy or with the support of others, advocating for your health needs is a critical step toward receiving respectful, competent, and personalized care.

8.3 Building a Positive Relationship with Your Healthcare Provider

Establishing a positive and constructive relationship with your healthcare provider is pivotal for effective healthcare management, particularly for individuals experiencing White Coat Syndrome or any form of health-related anxiety. A strong patient-provider relationship enhances communication, fosters trust, and improves health outcomes by ensuring that care is tailored to the patient's needs and concerns. This subchapter outlines strategies for building and maintaining a positive relationship with your healthcare provider, highlighting the mutual benefits of such a partnership.

Open and Honest Communication:

- **Be Transparent:** Share your medical history, symptoms, lifestyle habits, and any concerns or fears you have about your health or treatments. Honest communication provides a solid foundation for your care.

- **Express Your Feelings:** If you're feeling anxious or scared about a procedure or diagnosis, let your provider know. Recognizing your emotions can help them tailor their approach to your care.

Active Participation in Your Care:

- **Ask Questions:** Never hesitate to ask questions about your condition, treatment options, potential side effects, or any part of your care plan you don't fully understand. Asking questions not only clarifies your understanding but also shows your engagement in your healthcare.

- **Provide Feedback:** Give feedback about what's working and what isn't in your treatment plan. Your healthcare provider can use this information to adjust your care to better suit your needs.

Educate Yourself:

- **Understand Your Condition:** Use reputable sources to learn about your condition and treatment options. This knowledge enables you to engage in more meaningful discussions with your healthcare provider.

- **Know Your Rights:** Familiarize yourself with patient rights and responsibilities within the healthcare system. Understanding these can empower you to advocate for yourself effectively.

Respect and Courtesy:

- **Value Each Other's Time:** Be punctual for appointments and understand that healthcare providers often have tight schedules. If you need more time to discuss your concerns, mention this when scheduling your appointment.

- **Appreciate Their Expertise:** While it's essential to be an active participant in your care, also respect the knowledge and expertise of your healthcare provider. They can offer valuable insights and guidance based on their experience.

Follow Through on Recommendations:

- **Adhere to Treatment Plans:** Following your healthcare provider's recommendations and prescribed treatments demonstrates your commitment to managing your health. If you encounter difficulties with your treatment plan, communicate these challenges rather than discontinuing the therapy on your own.

Building Trust Over Time:

- **Consistency Is Key:** Building a positive relationship with your healthcare provider is a process that takes time. Consistent interactions based on mutual respect and open communication gradually foster a strong, trusting relationship.

- **Choose the Right Provider for You:** Sometimes, despite your best efforts, you may not click with a particular provider. It's okay to seek a different provider who better aligns with your communication style and needs.

Conclusion:

A positive relationship with your healthcare provider is instrumental in managing not just White Coat Syndrome but any health-related concerns. Such a relationship encourages a collaborative approach to healthcare, where the patient feels valued, heard, and actively involved in their care decisions. By employing the strategies outlined above, patients can contribute to building a productive partnership with their healthcare providers, leading to improved health outcomes and a more satisfying healthcare experience.

8.4 Exercise: 10 MCQs with Answers at the End

This exercise aims to consolidate your understanding of navigating healthcare settings, the significance of patient rights and advocacy, and strategies for building a positive relationship with healthcare providers, all crucial for managing health-related anxiety effectively.

Questions:

1. Effective communication with your healthcare provider includes:

   A. Only sharing symptoms you think are relevant.

B. Withholding information about your medical history to save time.

C. Being transparent about your health, symptoms, and concerns.

D. Avoiding questions not to challenge the provider's expertise.

2. Patient rights in healthcare typically include the right to:

A. Refuse any form of treatment without explanation.

B. Informed consent regarding treatment options and risks.

C. Unlimited access to experimental treatments.

D. Privacy, except in cases of public interest.

3. A positive patient-provider relationship is characterized by:

A. The patient's passive acceptance of all medical advice.

B. Mutual respect and open communication.

C. The provider makes all health decisions for the patient.

D. Infrequent communication to avoid burdening the provider.

4. The role of patient advocacy can involve:

A. Taking legal action against healthcare providers regularly.

B. Helping patients understand their rights and healthcare options.

C. Encouraging patients to self-diagnose using online resources.

D. Discouraging patients from asking questions during appointments.

5. Asking questions and providing feedback to your healthcare provider helps to:

A. Undermine the provider's confidence.

B. Improve the quality of care by ensuring it meets your needs.

C. Overload the provider with unnecessary information.

D. Avoid taking responsibility for your health.

6. Understanding your health insurance plan is essential because:

A. It allows you to bypass standard healthcare protocols.

B. You can avoid all healthcare costs.

C. It helps you know what services are covered and manage expenses.

D. Insurance details are required for all medical appointments.

7. Preparing for healthcare visits by writing down health concerns:

A. It Is unnecessary if you have a good memory.

B. Can ensure that all your concerns are addressed.

C. May overwhelm your healthcare provider.

D. Is discouraged to avoid anxiety.

8. Bringing a support person to medical appointments:

   A. Is generally frowned upon in healthcare settings.

   B. Can provide emotional support and help remember information.

   C. Is only beneficial for children and older people.

   D. May violate patient privacy laws.

9. Educating yourself about your condition and treatment options:

   A. Should be avoided to prevent self-misdiagnosis.

   B. Can empower you to make informed decisions about your care.

   C. Is the sole responsibility of your healthcare provider.

   D. Can lead to unnecessary anxiety and confusion.

10. The importance of following through on healthcare provider recommendations is to:

    A. Limit the provider's liability in your care.

    B. Demonstrate compliance without understanding the rationale.

    C. Improve health outcomes and address your concerns.

    D. Simplify the provider's job by not requiring further consultation.

Answers:

1. C. Being transparent about your health, symptoms, and concerns.

2. B. Informed consent regarding treatment options and risks.

3. B. Mutual respect and open communication.

4. B. Helping patients understand their rights and healthcare options.

5. B. Improve the quality of care by ensuring it meets your needs.

6. C. It helps you know what services are covered and manage expenses.

7. B. Can ensure that all your concerns are addressed.

8. B. It can provide emotional support and help remember information.

9. B. It can empower you to make informed decisions about your care.

10. C. Improve health outcomes and address your concerns.

These questions underscore the importance of active participation in healthcare, understanding patient rights, and the benefits of establishing a positive relationship with healthcare providers for managing health-related anxiety.

Chapter 9: Alternative Therapies

9.1 The Role of Acupuncture

Acupuncture, a key component of traditional Chinese medicine, has been practiced for thousands of years. It involves the insertion of skinny needles through the skin at strategic points on the body. Acupuncture is used for various purposes, from reducing pain to alleviating stress and anxiety, including the symptoms associated with White Coat Syndrome. This subchapter explores the role of acupuncture in managing health-related anxiety, its potential benefits, and what individuals can expect from this form of alternative therapy.

Understanding Acupuncture and Anxiety Management:

- **Mechanism:** Acupuncture is believed to stimulate the body's natural painkillers and increase the flow of energy or Qi. It may also impact the body's stress response system, reducing the production of stress hormones.

- **Evidence:** Research suggests acupuncture can help in managing symptoms of anxiety. It's thought to alter brain chemistry by changing the release of neurotransmitters and neurohormones in a way that positively affects mood and stress levels.

Potential Benefits of Acupuncture for Anxiety:

- **Reduction in Anxiety Symptoms:** Many patients report a significant reduction in feelings of anxiety and an enhanced sense of well-being after acupuncture sessions.

- **Improvement in Sleep:** Acupuncture can contribute to better sleep quality, which is often compromised in individuals dealing with anxiety.

- **Non-Pharmacological Approach:** For those seeking alternatives to medication, acupuncture offers a non-pharmacological method to manage anxiety with minimal side effects.

What to Expect During an Acupuncture Session:

- **Initial Assessment:** The practitioner will conduct a comprehensive assessment of your health history and symptoms to tailor the treatment to your specific needs.

- **Treatment Plan:** Based on the assessment, a treatment plan will be developed. The number of sessions required can vary depending on the individual's response to treatment.

- **Procedure:** During the session, thin needles are inserted into specific acupuncture points. While insertion may cause a slight prickling sensation, the procedure is generally not painful.

- **Relaxation:** Many people find acupuncture sessions relaxing and may even fall asleep during the treatment.

Choosing an Acupuncturist:

- **Certification and Licensing:** Ensure the practitioner is certified and licensed to practice acupuncture. Licensing requirements vary by region, so check the regulations in your area.

- **Specialization:** Look for practitioners who have experience or specialize in treating anxiety to ensure they understand your specific needs.

- **Consultation:** Consider scheduling a consultation with the practitioner to discuss your concerns and goals before starting treatment.

Considerations and Safety:

- **Safety:** Acupuncture is considered safe when performed by a qualified practitioner using sterile needles. Complications are rare but can include infections or injury if not correctly administered.

- **Complementary Therapy:** While acupuncture can be an effective tool for managing anxiety, it's often most beneficial when used as part of a comprehensive treatment plan that may include traditional therapies, lifestyle adjustments, and other complementary treatments.

Conclusion:

Acupuncture offers a promising alternative or complementary approach to managing health-related anxiety, including White Coat Syndrome. By potentially reducing anxiety symptoms, improving sleep, and offering a non-pharmacological treatment option, acupuncture can play a significant role in a holistic approach to anxiety management. As with any alternative therapy, it's essential to seek treatment from qualified professionals and consider acupuncture as one component of a broader health management strategy.

9.2 Benefits of Massage Therapy

Massage therapy, a practice rooted in ancient traditions, involves manipulating the body's soft tissues with techniques like kneading, rubbing, and pressing. It's widely recognized not only for its physical benefits but also for its effectiveness in reducing stress and anxiety, including the heightened anxiety associated with White Coat Syndrome. This subchapter delves into the benefits of massage therapy in managing health-related anxiety, highlighting how it can serve as a complementary approach to traditional medical treatments.

Physical and Psychological Benefits:

- **Stress Reduction:** One of the most immediate effects of massage therapy is a profound sense of relaxation and reduction in stress levels, attributed to the lowering of cortisol, the body's primary stress hormone.

- **Improved Sleep:** By promoting relaxation, massage therapy can also improve sleep quality, which is often negatively impacted by anxiety and stress. Better sleep contributes to improved overall well-being and mental health.

- **Enhanced Circulation:** Massage techniques can enhance blood circulation, facilitating the delivery of oxygen and nutrients to cells while aiding in the removal of waste products. This improved circulation can have a calming effect on the body.

- **Pain Relief:** For individuals whose anxiety is compounded by chronic pain, massage therapy can offer significant relief, thereby indirectly addressing one of the potential triggers of stress.

- **Increased Endorphin Levels:** Massage therapy can increase the body's production of endorphins, the natural chemicals associated with feelings of happiness and well-being, which can help counteract feelings of anxiety.

Massage Therapy for Anxiety Management:

- **Reducing Muscle Tension:** Anxiety often manifests physically as muscle tension or pain. Massage therapy can alleviate this tension, helping to reduce the physical symptoms associated with anxiety.

- **Mind-Body Connection:** Massage encourages mindfulness and a focus on the present moment. This mindfulness can help break the cycle of anxiety and stress by fostering a state of mental relaxation that complements the physical relaxation of the muscles.

- **Customizable Approaches:** Various forms of massage therapy, including Swedish, deep tissue, and aromatherapy massage, offer different approaches to relaxation and can be tailored to individual preferences and needs.

Considerations for Integrating Massage Therapy:

- **Consultation with Healthcare Providers:** Before incorporating massage therapy into your anxiety management plan, consult with your healthcare provider, especially if you have underlying health conditions.

- **Finding a Qualified Therapist:** Ensure that the massage therapist is licensed and has experience in working with clients who have anxiety. A therapist who understands your specific needs can tailor the session to maximize benefits.

- **Frequency and Duration:** The frequency and duration of massage therapy sessions can vary based on individual needs and responses. Discuss with your therapist to determine an appropriate schedule.

Conclusion:

Massage therapy offers a holistic approach to managing health-related anxiety, providing both physical and psychological benefits. By reducing stress, improving sleep, and addressing physical manifestations of anxiety, massage therapy can significantly enhance the quality of life for individuals dealing with White Coat Syndrome and other forms of anxiety. As part of a comprehensive treatment plan, massage therapy can complement traditional medical treatments and other lifestyle adjustments aimed at reducing stress.

9.3 Herbal Supplements and Their Efficacy

Herbal supplements have been used for centuries as natural remedies for a variety of ailments, including anxiety and stress. In recent years, there has been a growing interest in the potential of these supplements to offer a complementary approach to managing health-related anxiety, including conditions like White Coat Syndrome. This subchapter examines some commonly used herbal supplements for anxiety, their potential benefits, and considerations regarding their efficacy and safety.

Common Herbal Supplements for Anxiety:

- **Chamomile:** Often consumed as a tea, chamomile is known for its calming effects, which may help reduce symptoms of anxiety. It is thought to work by increasing levels of neurotransmitters associated with relaxation.

- **Valerian Root:** Valerian root is commonly used to improve sleep quality and reduce anxiety. It is believed to interact with gamma-aminobutyric acid (GABA), a chemical messenger that helps regulate nerve impulses in your brain and nervous system.

- **Lavender:** Lavender oil, used in aromatherapy or oral lavender supplements, has been shown to have a calming effect, potentially reducing anxiety levels.

- **Passionflower:** Passionflower is another herb thought to increase GABA levels in the brain, promoting relaxation and potentially easing anxiety symptoms.

- **St. John's Wort:** Primarily known for its use in treating depression, St. John's Wort may also have benefits for anxiety. However, its interactions with other medications necessitate caution.

Efficacy and Research:

- The efficacy of herbal supplements in treating anxiety varies, with research ranging from supportive to inconclusive. While many individuals report significant benefits, scientific studies have produced mixed results.

- Some supplements, like lavender and chamomile, have a substantial body of research supporting their use in reducing anxiety, while others require further study to understand their impact fully.

Safety and Considerations:

- **Interactions with Medications:** Herbal supplements can interact with prescription medications, potentially reducing effectiveness or causing adverse effects. It is crucial to consult with a healthcare provider before starting any herbal supplement.

- **Quality and Dosage:** The quality of herbal supplements can vary significantly between brands. Opt for products from reputable manufacturers and follow recommended dosages.

- **Individual Responses:** People may respond differently to herbal supplements. What works for one individual may not work for another, and some people may experience side effects.

Regulation and Oversight:

- In many regions, herbal supplements are not as tightly regulated as prescription medications, leading to potential variability in quality and concentration. Always research and choose products from reputable sources.

- Be wary of claims that seem too good to be true. Supplements that claim to work, like prescription anxiety medications, should be approached with caution.

Conclusion:

Herbal supplements can offer a complementary approach to managing anxiety for some individuals. However, their effectiveness can vary, and it's important to approach their use with an informed perspective, considering both potential benefits and risks. Consulting with healthcare professionals can help ensure that any supplement use is part of a comprehensive, safe, and effective plan for managing health-related anxiety, including White Coat Syndrome.

9.4 Exercise: 10 MCQs with Answers at the End

Test your understanding of alternative therapies for managing health-related anxiety, focusing on the role of acupuncture, the benefits of massage therapy, the efficacy of herbal supplements, and their overall impact on well-being.

Questions:

1. Acupuncture is believed to reduce anxiety by:

    A. Increasing physical pain tolerance.

    B. Altering the body's stress response system.

    C. Decreasing blood flow to the brain.

    D. Stimulating muscle growth.

2. Which herbal supplement is known for its calming effects and is often consumed as tea?

    A. Valerian Root

    B. Chamomile

C. Lavender

D. St. John's Wort

3. Massage therapy can help manage anxiety by:

   A. Increasing cortisol levels.

   B. Promoting relaxation and reducing stress hormone levels.

   C. Encouraging a sedentary lifestyle.

   D. Limiting blood circulation.

4. The primary mechanism by which Valerian Root is thought to reduce anxiety is:

   A. Suppressing the immune system.

   B. Increasing levels of GABA in the brain.

   C. Decreasing oxygen levels in the blood.

   D. Enhancing alertness.

5. One of the potential benefits of using lavender to manage anxiety is:

   A. Its ability to increase energy levels.

   B. The stimulation of appetite.

   C. Its calming effect.

   D. Improvement of vision.

6. St. John's Wort is primarily known for treating:

   A. High blood pressure.

   B. Depression and possibly anxiety.

   C. Muscle spasms.

   D. Bone fractures.

7. A key consideration when using herbal supplements for anxiety is:

   A. They can be used freely with any medication without concern for interactions.

   B. Their effects are immediate and long-lasting.

   C. There is a need to consult with a healthcare provider due to potential interactions with medications.

   D. They are regulated with the same rigor as prescription medications.

8. Passionflower is thought to ease anxiety symptoms by:

   A. Cooling the body temperature.

   B. Increasing GABA levels in the brain.

   C. Reducing the absorption of vitamins and minerals.

   D. Enhancing physical strength.

9. Regular physical activity aids in reducing anxiety by:

   A. Promoting a hyperactive state.

   B. Releasing endorphins, natural mood lifters.

   C. Decreasing lung capacity.

   D. Restricting blood flow to the brain.

10. In acupuncture, the strategic insertion of needles is believed to:

   A. Induce a state of physical discomfort to distract from anxiety.

   B. Decrease the effectiveness of the immune system.

   C. Increase the flow of energy or Qi and reduce stress hormone production.

   D. Block all sensations in treated areas.

Answers:

1. B. Altering the body's stress response system.

2. B. Chamomile

3. B. Promoting relaxation and reducing stress hormone levels.

4. B. Increasing levels of GABA in the brain.

5. C. Its calming effect.

6. B. Depression and possibly anxiety.

7. C. There is a need to consult with a healthcare provider due to potential interactions with medications.

8. B. Increasing GABA levels in the brain.

9. B. Releasing endorphins, natural mood lifters.

10. C. Increase the flow of energy or Qi and reduce stress hormone production.

These questions are designed to enhance your understanding of how alternative therapies like acupuncture, massage therapy, and herbal supplements can be integrated into a comprehensive approach to managing health-related anxiety, emphasizing the importance of consultation with healthcare providers to ensure safety and efficacy.

Chapter 10: Children and White Coat Syndrome

10.1 Recognizing Signs in Children

White Coat Syndrome, characterized by anxiety and stress in medical settings, is not exclusive to adults. Children, too, can experience heightened nervousness or fear during doctor visits or when facing medical procedures. Recognizing the signs of White Coat Syndrome in children is crucial for parents and caregivers to provide the necessary support and interventions. This subchapter focuses on identifying the symptoms of White Coat Syndrome in children and understanding how it may manifest differently compared to adults.

Common Signs of White Coat Syndrome in Children:

- **Verbal Expressions of Fear:** Children may express fear or anxiety about the doctor or hospital visits verbally. Phrases like "I don't want to go" or questions about whether the visit will hurt are common.

- **Physical Symptoms:** Similar to adults, children may exhibit physical symptoms of anxiety, such as stomachaches, headaches, or nausea, especially as the appointment approaches.

- **Behavioral Changes:** Look for changes in behavior, such as increased clinginess, crying, or tantrums, particularly when discussing medical visits or once in the medical setting.

- **Avoidance:** Older children might try to avoid medical appointments by making excuses or faking illness.

- **Elevated Vital Signs:** Just as with adults, children's blood pressure and heart rate may increase in a medical setting, even if they usually have readings within the normal range.

Understanding Children's Anxiety in Medical Settings:

- **Fear of the Unknown:** Much of the anxiety stems from not knowing what to expect. Children who are unfamiliar with medical procedures or environments may imagine the worst.

- **Past Experiences:** Previous negative experiences in healthcare settings can leave a lasting impression, leading to anticipatory anxiety about future visits.

- **Separation Anxiety:** Particularly in young children, fear of being separated from a parent during a medical examination or procedure can exacerbate feelings of anxiety.

Strategies for Parents and Caregivers:

- **Preparation and Education:** Use age-appropriate explanations to prepare children for what to expect during a medical visit. Books, videos, and role-playing can be practical tools.

- **Reassurance:** Provide constant reassurance that they are safe and that medical professionals are there to help them feel better.

- **Positive Reinforcement:** Praise and reward children for bravery and cooperation during medical visits.

- **Involve Children in the Process:** Allowing children to ask questions and express their fears can help them feel more in control.

- **Seek Professional Help if Needed:** If a child's anxiety about medical visits is severe or interferes with their ability to receive care, consider consulting a child psychologist or counselor who specializes in anxiety.

Conclusion:

Recognizing the signs of White Coat Syndrome in children and understanding the root causes of their anxiety are the first steps toward helping them cope. By employing strategies focused on preparation, reassurance, and positive reinforcement, parents and caregivers can significantly reduce the stress associated with medical visits for children. Establishing a foundation of positive healthcare experiences from a young age is crucial for promoting a lifelong approach to proactive health management.

10.2 Preparing a Child for a Doctor's Visit

Preparing a child for a doctor's visit is crucial in minimizing anxiety and ensuring a positive experience. This preparation can help mitigate White Coat Syndrome in children, making healthcare encounters less stressful for both the child and the caregiver. Adequate preparation involves informing, reassuring, and engaging the child in a way that's appropriate for their age and understanding. This subchapter outlines strategies to prepare a child for a doctor's visit, focusing on reducing fear and building confidence.

Educate About the Purpose:

- **Explain Why Visits Are Necessary:** Use simple, age-appropriate language to explain why the doctor's visit is essential. Emphasize that the doctor is there to help them stay healthy or get better.

- **Describe What to Expect:** Give a basic rundown of what might happen during the visit, including waiting, being measured and weighed, and the doctor's examination. Avoiding surprises can help reduce anxiety.

Use Positive Language:

- **Focus on Positives:** Highlight positive aspects of the visit, such as getting to know how their body works or getting a sticker after the appointment.

- **Avoid Negative Language:** Be cautious not to use the visit as a threat or punishment. Avoid phrases like "If you don't behave, the doctor will give you a shot."

Role-Play and Practice:

- **Doctor Play:** Use toys to simulate a doctor's visit, letting the child play with both the doctor and the patient. This can make the medical environment more familiar and less intimidating.

- **Practice Situations:** If possible, practice situations they might encounter, such as how to open their mouth wide for a throat exam or sit still for a blood pressure cuff.

Provide Reassurance and Support:

- **Assure Them of Your Presence:** Reassure your child that you'll be with them throughout the visit. Knowing they won't be alone can provide great comfort.

- **Address Fears:** Listen to your child's concerns and fears about the visit and address them directly with reassurance and factual information.

Involve Them in the Process:

- **Let Them Make Choices:** Where possible, let your child make choices related to the visit, such as which toy to bring along or which arm to use for the blood pressure test.

- **Encourage Questions:** Encourage your child to think of questions they might want to ask the doctor, reinforcing their sense of control and involvement.

Prepare Yourself:

- **Stay Calm:** Children often pick up on their caregivers' emotions. Try to stay calm and optimistic about the visit to help ease your child's fears.

- **Know the Details:** Be clear about the appointment's purpose, and have your questions or concerns ready to discuss with the doctor.

After the Visit:

- **Discuss the Experience:** Talk about the visit afterward, focusing on the positive aspects and how your child handled it. This can help reinforce a positive outlook for future visits.

- **Provide Praise and Reward:** Acknowledge your child's bravery or good behavior during the visit with praise or a small reward.

Conclusion:

Preparing a child for a doctor's visit is a proactive step that can significantly reduce anxiety and make healthcare experiences more positive. Through education, reassurance, and engagement, caregivers can help children feel more comfortable and confident about medical visits, laying the groundwork for healthier attitudes toward healthcare in the future.

10.3 Pediatric Care: Special Considerations

Pediatric care involves unique considerations to ensure that children receive not only the medical attention they need but also the emotional support necessary to navigate healthcare experiences positively. Children are not just small adults; their physical, emotional, and developmental needs require a specialized approach to care. This subchapter highlights critical aspects of pediatric care that healthcare providers and caregivers should consider to optimize outcomes and minimize anxiety for children facing medical environments, such as those with White Coat Syndrome.

Understanding Developmental Stages:

- **Tailored Communication:** Healthcare providers should adjust their communication style based on the child's age and developmental stage. This involves using age-appropriate language and explanations and engaging children directly in conversations about their health.

- **Respect Growing Independence:** For older children and adolescents, it's essential to respect their growing need for independence and privacy, allowing them opportunities to speak with healthcare providers on their own if they choose.

Creating a Child-Friendly Environment:

- **Welcoming Atmosphere:** Pediatric care settings should strive to be welcoming and child-friendly, with colorful decor, toys, and books available to make children feel more at ease.

- **Distraction Techniques:** Use of distraction techniques, such as playing music, using bubble blowers, or having the child watch videos during procedures, can significantly reduce anxiety and discomfort.

Involving Parents and Caregivers:

- **Active Participation:** Parents and caregivers should be actively involved in the child's care, providing comfort and reassurance throughout medical procedures and visits.

- **Education and Support:** Healthcare providers should educate parents on how to prepare their child for visits, recognize signs of anxiety, and support their child's emotional well-being.

Pain Management and Minimization:

- **Gentle Techniques:** Employing the gentlest techniques possible for medical procedures and making use of topical anesthetics or distraction can help minimize pain and distress.

- **Clear Explanations:** Explaining to children what they might feel during a procedure and reassuring them that it's okay to express discomfort can help prepare them mentally and reduce fear.

Emphasizing Preventive Care:

- **Routine Visits:** Encouraging regular well-child visits, not just appointments for illness, can help children become more comfortable with healthcare settings and view them as a regular part of staying healthy.

- **Vaccination Education:** Educating both parents and children about the importance of vaccinations and what to expect can help alleviate fears associated with shots.

Addressing Emotional Needs:

- **Recognizing Anxiety:** Healthcare providers should be attuned to signs of anxiety in children and have strategies ready to address these feelings, whether through conversation, play, or other comfort measures.

- **Support Services:** Referral to child psychologists or other mental health services should be considered for children who exhibit significant anxiety about medical care.

Conclusion:

Pediatric care requires a compassionate, informed approach that addresses the medical and emotional needs of children. By understanding developmental stages, creating a welcoming environment, involving parents, managing pain effectively, emphasizing preventive care, and addressing emotional needs, healthcare providers and caregivers can make medical experiences as positive as possible for children. This approach not only helps manage immediate concerns like White Coat Syndrome but also lays the foundation for a lifetime of positive healthcare interactions.

10.4 Exercise: 10 MCQs with Answers at the End

Evaluate your understanding of the critical concepts related to children and White Coat Syndrome, including recognizing signs, preparing for doctor's visits, pediatric care considerations, and practical strategies for managing healthcare anxiety in children.

Questions:

1. Recognizing signs of White Coat Syndrome in children often involves observing:

   A. Increased appetite before medical visits.

   B. Excitement about going to the doctor.

   C. Physical symptoms like stomachaches or headaches.

   D. Improved sleep patterns before appointments.

2. An effective way to prepare a child for a doctor's visit includes:

   A. Avoiding discussions about the visit to prevent anxiety.

   B. Explaining what will happen using age-appropriate language.

   C. Telling the child the visit will not hurt, regardless of procedures.

   D. Waiting until the last minute to inform them about the visit.

3. Pediatric care considerations should always include:

   A. Discouraging questions from children to keep visits short.

   B. Tailoring communication to the child's developmental stage.

   C. Using the same approach for children of all ages.

   D. Keeping parents out of the examination room to foster independence.

4. To create a child-friendly environment in healthcare settings, it is helpful to:

   A. Decorate rooms in neutral colors to minimize distractions.

   B. Offer toys and books that are age-appropriate.

   C. Ensure that the environment is as silent as possible.

   D. Avoid any child-specific decor to cater to all ages.

5. Distraction techniques during medical procedures may include:

   A. Ignoring the child's concerns to complete the procedure quickly.

   B. Having the child watch videos or listen to music.

   C. Discouraging the child from crying or expressing fear.

   D. Limiting the use of topical anesthetics to teach resilience.

6. When involving parents and caregivers in pediatric care, it is essential to:

   A. Only communicate with them and not directly with the child.

   B. Encourage active participation and provide comfort.

   C. Advise them to stay silent during visits so as not to confuse the child.

   D. Recommend they wait outside to promote the child's independence.

7. Addressing the emotional needs of children in healthcare settings can include:

   A. Minimizing the seriousness of their anxiety.

   B. Offering support services such as referrals to child psychologists.

   C. Telling them that other children are braver.

   D. Avoiding any discussions that could lead to emotional distress.

8. The role of preventive care in pediatric settings is to:

   A. Only address issues as they arise, not proactively.

   B. Help children become more comfortable with healthcare environments.

   C. Discourage regular visits to minimize exposure to germs.

   D. Limit discussions about vaccinations to avoid fear.

9. Effective pain management for children during medical procedures might involve:

   A. Using the most assertive possible techniques to ensure efficiency.

   B. Explain the procedure and use gentle techniques.

   C. Avoiding the use of any pain relief to quicken the process.

   D. Withholding information about possible discomfort.

10. An essential aspect of pediatric care is:

   A. Ensuring children understand the long-term implications of their health.

   B. Tailoring the approach to meet the physical and emotional needs of each child.

   C. Treating children the same as adult patients to prepare them for the future.

   D. Encouraging self-care practices without parental involvement.

Answers:

1. C. Physical symptoms like stomachaches or headaches.

2. B. Explaining what will happen using age-appropriate language.

3. B. Tailoring communication to the child's developmental stage.

4. B. Offer toys and books that are age-appropriate.

5. B. Have the child watch videos or listen to music.

6. B. Encourage active participation and provide comfort.

7. B. Offering support services such as referrals to child psychologists.

8. B. Help children become more comfortable with healthcare environments.

9. B. Explain the procedure and use gentle techniques.

10. B. Tailoring the approach to meet the physical and emotional needs of each child.

These questions and answers are designed to reinforce the importance of recognizing and addressing White Coat Syndrome in children, ensuring their healthcare experiences are as positive and supportive as possible.

Chapter 11: The Future of Patient Care

11.1 Innovations in Reducing Patient Anxiety

The landscape of patient care is evolving rapidly, with new technologies and approaches being developed to reduce patient anxiety, enhance the patient experience, and improve overall health outcomes. Innovations in healthcare aim to address common concerns such as White Coat Syndrome by creating more patient-friendly environments, utilizing digital tools for education and engagement, and personalizing care. This subchapter explores some of the most promising innovations designed to reduce patient anxiety.

Virtual Reality (VR) and Augmented Reality (AR):

- **Immersive Experiences for Relaxation:** VR and AR can transport patients to calming environments or provide guided meditation experiences, reducing anxiety before and during medical procedures.

- **Educational Tools:** These technologies can also be used to educate patients about their conditions and treatments in an interactive, engaging manner, helping to demystify medical procedures and reduce fear of the unknown.

Telehealth and Digital Communication Platforms:

- **Remote Consultations:** Telehealth allows patients to consult with healthcare providers from the comfort of their homes, reducing stress associated with visiting medical facilities.

- **Enhanced Communication:** Secure messaging platforms and patient portals facilitate better communication between patients and healthcare providers, allowing for timely advice, reassurance, and support.

Wearable Health Technology:

- **Real-Time Health Monitoring:** Wearable devices can monitor vital signs and stress indicators, providing patients and healthcare providers with valuable data to manage health proactively and reduce anxiety about unknown health statuses.

- **Biofeedback and Stress Management:** Some wearables offer biofeedback mechanisms, teaching patients how to control physiological functions such as heart rate, potentially reducing anxiety.

Personalized Medicine:

- **Genetic Profiling and Tailored Treatments:** Advances in genetics and personalized medicine ensure treatments are specifically tailored to the individual's genetic makeup, reducing trial and error in medication selection and increasing the effectiveness of treatments.

- **Predictive Analytics:** Utilizing data analytics to predict potential health issues before they become serious can reduce anxiety by allowing for early intervention and management.

Artificial Intelligence (AI) and Machine Learning:

- **Diagnostic Support:** AI can assist in diagnosing diseases more quickly and accurately, reducing the anxious waiting period for patients.

- **Therapeutic Chatbots:** AI-driven chatbots can provide immediate support and counseling services, offering coping strategies and immediate reassurance outside of regular healthcare provider hours.

Environmental Design in Healthcare Settings:

- **Healing Environments:** Architectural and interior design strategies that create calming, healing environments in healthcare settings can significantly impact reducing patient anxiety. This includes the use of natural light, green spaces, and private, comfortable patient areas.

- **Child-Friendly Spaces:** For pediatric care, environments that are colorful, engaging, and designed with children in mind can make medical facilities less intimidating and more welcoming.

Conclusion:

The future of patient care looks promising, with innovations focusing on reducing patient anxiety, enhancing the efficiency and effectiveness of treatments, and improving the overall healthcare experience. By embracing these advancements, healthcare providers can create a more supportive, understanding, and patient-centered care environment. These innovations not only aim to reduce immediate anxiety but also foster a long-term positive relationship between patients and the healthcare system, ultimately leading to better health outcomes and a more compassionate approach to healthcare.

11.2 The Role of Telemedicine

Telemedicine has emerged as a transformative force in healthcare, leveraging technology to deliver medical care remotely, thereby increasing accessibility and convenience and potentially reducing patient anxiety. It encompasses a range of services, including consultations, therapy sessions, monitoring chronic conditions, and even some aspects of emergency care. This subchapter explores the role of telemedicine in modern healthcare, particularly its impact on reducing patient anxiety and improving patient experiences.

Expanding Access to Care:

- **Geographical Reach:** Telemedicine breaks down geographical barriers, enabling patients in remote or underserved areas to access specialist care without the need to travel long distances.

- **Convenience:** Patients can receive care from the comfort of their homes, reducing the stress and inconvenience associated with traditional in-person visits.

Reducing Patient Anxiety:

- **Familiar Environment:** Receiving care in a familiar, comfortable setting can significantly reduce anxiety, especially for individuals with White Coat Syndrome or those who experience heightened stress in clinical environments.

- **Flexible Scheduling:** Telemedicine often offers greater flexibility in scheduling appointments, reducing the anxiety associated with fitting medical visits into busy schedules.

Enhancing Patient-Provider Communication:

- **Continuous Engagement:** Digital platforms allow for more frequent and direct communication between patients and healthcare providers, fostering a more potent therapeutic relationship.

- **Personalized Care:** The ease of communication can lead to more personalized care plans, as patients are more likely to report symptoms and concerns in real time.

Supporting Mental Health:

- **Teletherapy:** Telemedicine has been particularly effective in delivering mental health services, offering a discrete and accessible way for individuals to seek help for anxiety, depression, and other mental health issues.

- **Anxiety and Stress Management:** Many telemedicine platforms provide resources and programs specifically designed to help manage stress and anxiety, including guided meditation, breathing exercises, and cognitive-behavioral therapy techniques.

Considerations and Challenges:

- **Privacy and Security:** Ensuring the privacy and security of patient data is paramount, requiring robust digital safeguards to protect sensitive health information.

- **Technology Access and Literacy:** The effectiveness of telemedicine depends on patients having access to the necessary technology and being comfortable using it, which may be a barrier for some populations.

- **Regulatory and Reimbursement Issues:** The adoption of telemedicine is influenced by regulatory environments and insurance reimbursement policies, which vary widely across regions.

Conclusion:

Telemedicine represents a significant advancement in patient care, offering a viable alternative to traditional in-person visits that can reduce patient anxiety, improve access to care, and enhance the overall healthcare experience. As technology continues to evolve and integrate into healthcare systems, telemedicine is poised to play an increasingly central role in delivering effective, patient-centered care. By addressing the challenges and leveraging the opportunities presented by telemedicine, healthcare providers can ensure that all patients, regardless of location or circumstance, have access to the care they need.

11.3 Personalized Medicine and Patient Comfort

Personalized medicine represents a shift towards more tailored healthcare, where treatments and preventive strategies are customized to individual genetic, environmental, and lifestyle factors. This approach not only enhances the efficacy of treatments but also significantly improves patient comfort and reduces anxiety by ensuring that care is as effective and minimally invasive as possible. This subchapter explores the impact of personalized medicine on patient comfort and its role in alleviating healthcare-related anxieties, such as White Coat Syndrome.

Foundations of Personalized Medicine:

- **Genetic Profiling:** Advances in genomics allow for the identification of genetic markers that predict susceptibility to certain diseases, response to medications, and potential side effects, enabling more precise and effective treatments.

- **Environmental and Lifestyle Considerations:** Personalized medicine also takes into account an individual's environment and lifestyle, tailoring health recommendations and treatments to fit their unique context.

Benefits for Patient Comfort and Anxiety Reduction:

- **Targeted Treatments:** By focusing on the most effective treatments for an individual's specific condition, personalized medicine can reduce the trial and error often associated with traditional approaches, minimizing unnecessary side effects and stress.

- **Increased Efficacy:** Treatments that are specifically designed to work with an individual's genetic makeup are often more effective, leading to faster recovery times and less time spent dealing with ineffective treatments.

- **Empowered Patients:** Personalized medicine involves patients in their care decisions to a greater extent, providing them with information and options tailored to their unique needs. This empowerment can reduce feelings of helplessness and anxiety.

- **Proactive Health Management:** The use of predictive analytics in personalized medicine allows for earlier detection and prevention of disease, reducing the anxiety associated with uncertainty about future health.

Incorporating Personalized Medicine into Patient Care:

- **Collaboration Between Patients and Providers:** Effective personalized medicine requires open communication and collaboration, with patients sharing detailed information about their health history, lifestyle, and preferences.

- **Educational Resources:** Providing patients with resources to understand their genetic information and how it affects their health care can further reduce anxiety by demystifying complex concepts.

- **Integrating Technology:** Wearable devices and mobile health apps can monitor health indicators in real-time, providing data that supports personalized healthcare decisions and enhances patient engagement in their care.

Challenges and Considerations:

- **Accessibility:** Ensuring that personalized medicine is accessible to all patients, regardless of socioeconomic status, is crucial to avoid exacerbating health disparities.

- **Privacy Concerns:** The collection and analysis of genetic and personal health data raise significant privacy issues, requiring stringent protections to maintain patient trust.

Conclusion:

Personalized medicine offers a promising avenue for enhancing patient comfort and reducing healthcare-related anxiety. By focusing on the unique characteristics of each patient, healthcare providers can deliver more effective, efficient, and comfortable care, transforming the patient experience. As personalized medicine continues to evolve, it has the potential to impact how healthcare is delivered significantly, prioritizing not only the physical well-being of patients but also their emotional and psychological health.

11.4 Exercise: 10 MCQs with Answers at the End

This exercise is designed to assess your comprehension of the innovative strategies and approaches discussed in Chapter 11 for enhancing patient care, reducing anxiety, and improving the healthcare experience through technology, personalized medicine, and telemedicine.

Questions:

1. Virtual Reality (VR) in healthcare is primarily used to:

   A. Replace traditional treatments entirely.

   B. Provide immersive experiences for relaxation and education.

   C. Increase the need for in-person visits.

   D. Limit patient interaction with healthcare providers.

2. Telemedicine improves patient care by:

   A. Discouraging direct communication between patients and providers.

   B. Offering remote consultations, increasing access and convenience.

   C. Eliminating the need for physical examinations.

   D. Reducing the accuracy of diagnoses.

3. Wearable health technology aids in managing patient anxiety by:

   A. Monitoring vital signs and providing real-time health data.

   B. Decreasing patient engagement in their care.

   C. Replacing all other forms of medical treatment.

   D. Increasing the complexity of healthcare management.

4. Personalized medicine tailors treatments based on:

   A. The most common symptoms presented by patients.

   B. A patient's genetic profile, lifestyle, and environmental factors.

   C. Generalized treatment protocols.

   D. The availability of medications.

5. The role of AI and machine learning in healthcare include:

   A. Decreasing the efficiency of healthcare delivery.

   B. Providing diagnostic support and therapeutic chatbots.

   C. Complicating the patient care process.

   D. Reducing patient access to information.

6. The primary challenge in integrating telemedicine into patient care is:

   A. Ensuring privacy and security of patient data.

   B. Encouraging more frequent in-person visits.

   C. Limiting patient access to technology.

   D. Avoiding any form of patient education.

7. Environmental design in healthcare settings focuses on:

   A. Creating stressful and complex environments.

   B. Reducing patient comfort and increasing anxiety.

C. Creating calming, healing environments.

D. Discouraging personalization in patient rooms.

8. The significance of genetic profiling in personalized medicine is to:

A. Decrease the customization of healthcare plans.

B. Identify genetic markers that predict disease susceptibility and treatment response.

C. Ignore environmental and lifestyle factors.

D. Simplify treatment options to one-size-fits-all solutions.

9. Challenges of personalized medicine include:

A. Enhancing the patient-provider relationship.

B. Ensuring accessibility for all patients.

C. Reducing the need for patient education.

D. Minimizing the role of technology in healthcare.

10. A key benefit of using AR for patient education is:

A. Increasing confusion about medical conditions and treatments.

B. Engaging patients in an interactive, understandable manner.

C. Discouraging questions from patients during consultations.

D. Limiting the need for detailed explanations from healthcare providers.

Answers:

1. B. Provide immersive experiences for relaxation and education.

2. B. Offering remote consultations, increasing access and convenience.

3. A. Monitoring vital signs and providing real-time health data.

4. B. A patient's genetic profile, lifestyle, and environmental factors.

5. B. Providing diagnostic support and therapeutic chatbots.

6. A. Ensuring privacy and security of patient data.

7. C. Creating calming, healing environments.

8. B. Identify genetic markers that predict disease susceptibility and treatment response.

9. B. Ensuring accessibility for all patients.

10. B. Engaging patients in an interactive, understandable manner.

These questions highlight the importance of understanding the latest innovations in healthcare designed to improve patient experiences, reduce anxiety, and provide more effective, personalized care.

Chapter 12: Case Studies and Success Stories

12.1 Overcoming Severe White Coat Syndrome

This subchapter presents a case study illustrating the journey of a patient, Alex, who overcame severe White Coat Syndrome through a comprehensive and multidisciplinary approach. This story highlights the challenges faced by patients with intense healthcare-related anxiety and the strategies that can lead to successful management and reduction of this condition.

Background:

Alex, a 35-year-old with a history of avoiding medical settings due to severe anxiety, had not visited a doctor in over five years despite experiencing chronic headaches and occasional dizzy spells. The mere thought of making an appointment triggered intense anxiety, characterized by palpitations, sweating, and nausea.

Intervention Strategies:

1. Initial Engagement through Telemedicine:

- **Strategy:** To ease Alex into the healthcare system, their first consultation was conducted via telemedicine. This approach allowed Alex to meet their healthcare provider in a comfortable, familiar environment.

- **Outcome:** The remote consultation significantly reduced Alex's initial anxiety, enabling them to discuss their symptoms and concerns openly.

2. Gradual Exposure to In-Person Visits:

- **Strategy:** Following several telemedicine sessions, Alex and their provider agreed on a short, in-person visit focused solely on getting to know the clinic environment without undergoing any examinations.

- **Outcome:** These visits gradually desensitized Alex to the healthcare setting, reducing their anxiety about future appointments.

3. Behavioral Therapy:

- **Strategy:** Alex was referred to a psychologist specializing in cognitive-behavioral therapy (CBT) for anxiety. Through CBT, Alex learned to identify and challenge negative thought patterns related to healthcare settings and developed coping strategies for managing stress.

- **Outcome:** Over time, Alex's anxiety levels during healthcare visits significantly decreased, allowing them to attend appointments more regularly.

4. Use of Technology for Support:

- **Strategy:** Alex utilized a meditation app recommended by their psychologist to practice relaxation techniques before appointments and whenever they felt anxious about upcoming visits.

- **Outcome:** The app helped Alex manage their anxiety more effectively, providing a tool they could use in real-time to calm themselves.

5. Building a Supportive Healthcare Relationship:

- **Strategy:** Alex's healthcare provider made efforts to build a trusting relationship, ensuring open communication and actively involving Alex in decisions about their care.

- **Outcome:** Feeling heard and respected by their provider further reduced Alex's anxiety and fostered a positive attitude towards healthcare.

Success and Ongoing Management:

Over two years, Alex went from avoiding all medical settings to regularly attending necessary appointments and actively engaging in health management. They learned to manage their anxiety through a combination of behavioral strategies, technological support, and a solid patient-provider relationship.

Conclusion:

Alex's journey underscores the importance of a personalized and patient-centered approach to managing White Coat Syndrome. By addressing both the psychological and situational aspects of healthcare-related anxiety, patients like Alex can overcome their fears and engage proactively in their healthcare. This case study illustrates the potential for successful outcomes through the integration of telemedicine, psychological support, technology, and compassionate healthcare practices.

12.2 Innovative Approaches in Practice

This subchapter explores various innovative approaches that healthcare professionals and institutions have implemented to enhance patient care, explicitly targeting the reduction of patient anxiety and improving overall patient experiences. These real-world examples highlight the success of creative strategies in addressing healthcare challenges.

Case Study 1: Virtual Reality for Pediatric Patients

- **Background:** A children's hospital introduced Virtual Reality (VR) headsets for pediatric patients undergoing painful or anxiety-inducing procedures.

- **Approach:** Patients could choose from a variety of immersive, calming environments or interactive games to be engaged in during their procedure.

- **Outcome:** The use of VR significantly reduced procedure-related anxiety and pain perception among pediatric patients, leading to a more positive healthcare experience and faster procedures due to reduced movement and distress.

Case Study 2: Telehealth Integration in Mental Health Services

- **Background:** A mental health clinic integrated telehealth services to provide continuous support to patients with anxiety disorders, including those with severe healthcare-related anxiety.

- **Approach:** Patients received regular telehealth consultations and access to an online platform for self-management tools, including mood tracking, meditation guides, and direct messaging with their therapist.

- **Outcome:** The clinic reported higher patient engagement levels, reduced missed appointments, and significant improvements in anxiety management among patients, demonstrating the effectiveness of remote support and digital tools in mental health care.

Case Study 3: Pet Therapy in Oncology Units

- **Background:** An oncology unit introduced a pet therapy program where trained therapy dogs visited patients during their chemotherapy sessions.

- **Approach:** Patients had the opportunity to interact with therapy dogs, providing comfort and distraction from the stress of treatment.

- **Outcome:** The program was overwhelmingly positive, with patients reporting decreased anxiety and improved mood on treatment days. The presence of therapy dogs also facilitated social interaction among patients, creating a supportive community environment.

Case Study 4: Personalized Music Playlists During Surgery

- **Background:** A surgical center allowed patients to create personalized music playlists to listen to through headphones during awake procedures.

- **Approach:** Patients selected music that they found soothing or uplifting, which was then played for them during surgery to reduce anxiety and improve patient comfort.

- **Outcome:** Post-procedure surveys indicated a significant reduction in patient anxiety and pain perception, with many patients noting the music helped them feel more relaxed and distracted from the surgical environment.

Case Study 5: Designing Healing Environments

- **Background:** A hospital redesigned its patient rooms and common areas to incorporate elements of nature, such as indoor plants, natural light, and outdoor views, to create a more healing environment.

- **Approach:** The redesign focused on creating calm, restorative spaces that promote relaxation and reduce stress for patients and their families.

- **Outcome:** Patient satisfaction surveys showed a marked improvement in how patients felt about their hospital stay, with many citing the healing environment as a critical factor in their overall positive experience.

Conclusion:

These case studies exemplify how innovative approaches, leveraging technology, natural elements, and therapy animals, among others, can significantly impact reducing patient anxiety and enhancing the healthcare experience. By adopting creative solutions tailored to patient needs, healthcare providers can address the multifaceted challenges of patient care, leading to better outcomes and more positive perceptions of healthcare environments.

12.3 Long-Term Management and Recovery

Effective long-term management and recovery from health-related anxieties, such as White Coat Syndrome, require a comprehensive approach that addresses both the psychological and physical aspects of the condition. This subchapter explores strategies and practices that support sustained management and recovery, ensuring individuals can maintain their well-being and engage in healthcare proactively and positively over time.

Comprehensive Care Plans:

- **Integrated Care Approach:** Combining medical treatment with psychological support, such as cognitive-behavioral therapy (CBT) or mindfulness-based stress reduction (MBSR), offers a holistic strategy for managing anxiety.

- **Personalized Treatment:** Tailoring care plans to the individual's specific needs, preferences, and experiences enhances engagement and effectiveness, promoting long-term adherence and positive outcomes.

Lifestyle Modifications:

- **Regular Physical Activity:** Engaging in regular exercise has been shown to significantly reduce symptoms of anxiety and improve mood, acting as a natural stress reliever.

- **Healthy Diet:** A balanced diet, rich in nutrients and low in processed foods, can positively affect mental health, supporting anxiety management.

- **Adequate Sleep:** Ensuring sufficient and quality sleep is crucial for emotional regulation and stress management, impacting overall anxiety levels.

Continuous Support and Education:

- **Ongoing Therapy:** Continued access to psychological support helps individuals develop coping mechanisms for dealing with anxiety triggers and maintaining mental health.

- **Patient Education:** Providing patients with resources and education about their condition, treatment options, and anxiety management techniques empowers them to take control of their health.

Stress Management Techniques:

- **Mindfulness and Relaxation:** Practices such as meditation, yoga, and deep breathing exercises can help individuals manage stress and reduce anxiety in daily life.

- **Biofeedback and Neurofeedback:** These techniques teach individuals to control physiological processes related to stress, offering tools for anxiety management.

Building a Supportive Network:

- **Social Support:** Encouraging patients to cultivate a supportive network of family, friends, and peers can provide emotional comfort and practical assistance, reducing feelings of isolation.

- **Professional Networks:** Access to support groups or networks of individuals with similar experiences can offer camaraderie, shared tips for managing anxiety, and a sense of community.

Monitoring and Adjusting Care Plans:

- **Regular Assessments:** Periodic evaluations of the individual's mental health and the effectiveness of the care plan allow for adjustments as needed, ensuring the approach remains responsive to the patient's evolving needs.

- **Adaptability:** Flexibility in care strategies is crucial, as what works at one stage may need to be modified over time to adapt to changes in the individual's life, health status, or anxiety levels.

Conclusion:

Long-term management and recovery from health-related anxieties are achievable through a multi-faceted approach that includes comprehensive care, lifestyle modifications, continuous support, and personalized strategies. By addressing the condition from various angles and maintaining an adaptable, patient-centered care plan, individuals can experience significant improvements in their anxiety levels, quality of life, and engagement with healthcare. Success in long-term management fosters resilience, empowering patients to face healthcare experiences with confidence and reduced anxiety.

12.4 Exercise: 10 MCQs with Answers at the End

This exercise aims to reinforce critical concepts and strategies discussed in Chapter 12, focusing on overcoming White Coat Syndrome, innovative approaches in healthcare to reduce patient anxiety, and the importance of long-term management for sustained recovery and well-being.

Questions:

1. What is a holistic strategy for managing White Coat Syndrome?

   A. Avoiding all medical appointments

   B. Using only medication to manage anxiety

   C. Combining medical treatment with psychological support

   D. Focusing solely on symptom management

2. Tailoring care plans to individual needs enhances:

   A. Dependency on healthcare providers

   B. Short-term recovery only

   C. Engagement and Effectiveness

   D. Anxiety levels due to overwhelming choices

3. Regular exercise benefits individuals with health-related anxieties by:

   A. Increasing stress levels to build resilience

   B. Acting as a natural stress reliever

   C. Isolating them from social interactions

   D. Reducing the need for medical care

4. Continuous psychological support is essential for:

   A. Decreasing patient autonomy

   B. Developing coping mechanisms for anxiety triggers

   C. Limiting patient involvement in care decisions

   D. Encouraging reliance on medication

5. A balanced diet impacts mental health by:

   A. Increasing cravings for processed foods

   B. Positively affecting mood and stress management

C. Leading to weight gain that can increase anxiety

D. Reducing the effectiveness of anxiety treatments

6. Mindfulness and relaxation practices help manage stress by:

    A. Distracting from health-related issues

    B. Teaching control over physiological stress responses

    C. Increasing physical discomfort

    D. Encouraging passive coping strategies

7. The role of social support in managing health-related anxiety includes:

    A. Reinforcing negative health behaviors

    B. Providing emotional comfort and practical assistance

    C. Decreasing communication with healthcare providers

    D. Limiting exposure to different perspectives on health

8. Adaptability in care strategies is crucial because:

    A. Patients' health conditions do not change over time

    B. It prevents patients from fully recovering

    C. What works at one stage may need modification later

    D. Healthcare providers prefer a rigid approach to treatment

9. Virtual Reality (VR) reduces procedure-related anxiety in pediatric patients by:

   A. Replacing traditional pain management methods

   B. Providing immersive experiences for relaxation

   C. Limiting patient interaction with healthcare staff

   D. Increasing awareness of the medical environment

10. The integration of telehealth services in mental health care:

   A. Reduces patient engagement and increases missed appointments

   B. Offers discrete and accessible support for managing anxiety

   C. Discourages the use of self-management tools

   D. Decreases the accuracy of mental health diagnoses

Answers:

1. C. Combining medical treatment with psychological support

2. C. Engagement and Effectiveness

3. B. Acting as a natural stress reliever

4. B. Developing coping mechanisms for anxiety triggers

5. B. Positively affecting mood and stress management

6. B. Teaching control over physiological stress responses

7. B. Providing emotional comfort and practical assistance

8. C. What works at one stage may need modification later

9. B. Providing immersive experiences for relaxation

10. B. Offers discrete and accessible support for managing anxiety

These questions and answers highlight the multifaceted approaches to managing health-related anxieties, emphasizing the importance of comprehensive care plans, lifestyle adjustments, and the integration of innovative healthcare solutions for long-term well-being and recovery.

Chapter 13: Creating a Personal Action Plan

13.1 Setting Realistic Goals

Creating a personal action plan for managing health-related anxieties, such as White Coat Syndrome, begins with setting realistic and achievable goals. These goals serve as a roadmap, guiding individuals through the steps necessary to reduce anxiety, improve health outcomes, and foster a more positive relationship with healthcare settings. This subchapter provides insights into establishing realistic goals that are tailored to an individual's specific needs and circumstances.

Identifying Your Objectives:

- **Define Specific Targets:** Start by identifying what you want to achieve. This could range from attending regular healthcare appointments without excessive stress to actively participating in discussions with healthcare providers.

- **Understand Your Triggers:** Recognizing the specific aspects of healthcare settings or procedures that trigger anxiety is crucial. This understanding allows you to set goals aimed at addressing these triggers directly.

SMART Goals Framework:

- **Specific:** Make your goals as clear and detailed as possible. Instead of a general goal like "feel less anxious," specify what feeling less anxious means to you, such as "being able to measure my blood pressure without experiencing panic."

- **Measurable:** Ensure that you can track your progress towards your goal. For example, "Attend all scheduled healthcare appointments in the next six months."

- **Achievable:** Your goals should be realistic and attainable within your current circumstances and resources.

- **Relevant:** Choose goals that are meaningful and beneficial to your overall well-being and healthcare needs.

- **Time-bound:** Set a reasonable timeframe for achieving your goals to maintain focus and motivation.

Steps to Achieve Your Goals:

- **Break Down Goals:** Divide larger goals into smaller, manageable tasks. If your goal is to reduce anxiety during medical appointments, start with tasks like scheduling an appointment, visiting the healthcare facility without having a procedure or speaking with a healthcare provider via telehealth.

- **Develop Coping Strategies:** Identify techniques that can help manage anxiety, such as deep breathing exercises, mindfulness, or speaking with a therapist, and incorporate these into your action plan.

- **Seek Support:** Include seeking support from friends, family, or support groups as part of your action plan. Sharing your goals with others can provide additional motivation and accountability.

Monitoring Progress:

- **Keep a Journal:** Document your experiences, feelings, and any strategies you find compelling. This can help you track your progress and adjust your action plan as needed.

- **Celebrate Achievements:** Recognize and celebrate when you reach milestones, no matter how small. This reinforces positive behavior and keeps you motivated towards your larger goals.

Reevaluating and Adjusting Goals:

- **Flexibility:** Be prepared to adjust your goals based on your experiences and progress. What works initially may need to be modified as you grow and change.

- **Continuous Improvement:** View your action plan as a living document that evolves with you. Regularly reassessing and updating your goals ensures they remain aligned with your needs and aspirations.

Conclusion:

Setting realistic goals is the foundation of a personal action plan for managing health-related anxieties. By using the SMART framework, breaking goals into actionable steps, and continuously monitoring and adjusting your approach, you can make significant strides in overcoming fear and improving your healthcare experiences.

13.2 Monitoring Progress and Adjusting Strategies

Monitoring progress is a critical component of any personal action plan, especially when managing health-related anxieties such as White Coat Syndrome. Regularly assessing how well your strategies are working allows you to make necessary adjustments, ensuring that your approach remains effective over time. This subchapter guides you on how to monitor your progress and adjust your strategies to continue moving toward your goals.

Establishing Benchmarks for Success:

- **Set Clear Indicators:** Identify specific indicators of success based on your goals. For instance, if your goal is to reduce anxiety during healthcare visits, indicators might include a decrease in physical symptoms of anxiety and increased comfort in discussing health concerns with providers or attending appointments without significant distress.

- **Use a Journal or Tracking Tool:** Keeping a detailed record of your experiences, feelings, and any symptoms of anxiety can help you identify patterns and progress. Note what strategies were in place when you felt improvements or faced setbacks.

Regular Review and Reflection:

- **Schedule Regular Reviews:** Set aside time regularly (e.g., monthly or quarterly) to review your journal or tracking tool. Reflect on your progress towards your goals and the effectiveness of the strategies you've employed.

- **Involve a Support System:** Share your progress with a trusted friend, family member, or therapist. They can offer valuable outside perspectives on your growth and areas for improvement.

Adjusting Strategies Based on Feedback:

- **Be Open to Change:** If specific strategies aren't yielding the expected results, be willing to try new approaches. Flexibility is critical to finding what works best for you.

- **Incorporate New Techniques:** As you learn more about managing anxiety, you may come across new techniques or resources. Incorporate these into your plan as appropriate.

Overcoming Plateaus and Setbacks:

- **Identify Causes:** If progress stalls or you experience a setback, try to identify the cause. Was there a particular trigger or change in circumstances?

- **Adapt Your Plan:** Use setbacks as learning opportunities to refine your strategies. Adjusting your plan based on these experiences can help you overcome similar challenges in the future.

Celebrating Achievements:

- **Acknowledge Success:** Recognize and celebrate your achievements, no matter how small. Achieving milestones can provide motivation and reinforce the value of your efforts.

- **Reflect on Growth:** Take time to reflect on how far you've come from the start of your action plan. Acknowledging your growth can boost your confidence and commitment to ongoing management.

Seeking Professional Guidance:

- **Consult with Healthcare Providers:** Regular check-ins with your healthcare provider can offer professional insights into your progress and additional strategies for managing anxiety.

- **Therapy Sessions:** Continuing or revisiting therapy can provide support in refining coping strategies, especially when facing new challenges or significant stressors.

Conclusion:

Monitoring progress and adjusting strategies are dynamic processes that play a crucial role in the effective long-term management of health-related anxieties. By setting clear benchmarks, regularly reviewing progress, celebrating achievements, and being open to changing strategies as needed, individuals can continue to make strides in overcoming anxiety and improving their healthcare experiences.

13.3 Utilizing Resources and Support Systems

Successfully managing health-related anxieties, including White Coat Syndrome, often requires more than individual effort; it involves leveraging various resources and support systems. Accessing the right tools and engaging with supportive networks can significantly enhance the effectiveness of your personal action plan. This subchapter discusses how to identify and utilize resources and support systems to aid in the management of healthcare-related anxiety.

Identifying Helpful Resources:

- **Educational Materials:** Look for reputable sources of information that can help you understand your anxiety better, including books, websites, and online courses. Knowledge about anxiety and its management can empower you to take control of your condition.

- **Digital Tools:** Apps for meditation, mindfulness, and stress management can provide practical support in managing anxiety daily. Many of these tools offer guided exercises, tracking capabilities, and personalized feedback.

- **Professional Services:** Consider services offered by psychologists, counselors, or therapists specializing in anxiety disorders. Telehealth options can also make these services more accessible.

- **Community Support:** Support groups, either in-person or online, connect you with others facing similar challenges. These groups can offer empathy, shared experiences, and coping strategies.

Building a Supportive Network:

- **Family and Friends:** Openly communicate with your family and friends about your anxiety and how they can support you. Specific ways they can help might include accompanying you to appointments or simply being there to listen.

- **Healthcare Providers:** Establish a collaborative relationship with your healthcare providers. Feel comfortable asking questions, expressing concerns, and discussing your anxiety openly with them.

- **Peer Support:** Connecting with peers who have successfully managed their healthcare-related anxiety can provide hope and practical advice. Peer mentors can share their strategies and insights from their own experiences.

Leveraging Community and Online Resources:

- **Local Workshops and Seminars:** Many communities offer workshops or seminars focused on stress management, mindfulness, and other relevant topics. These can be great opportunities to learn new strategies and meet others who are working to manage their anxiety.

- **Online Forums and Social Media:** Online communities can offer support and advice 24/7. These platforms allow you to share your experiences and learn from others in a flexible and accessible format.

Maintaining Engagement with Your Support System:

- **Regular Check-ins:** Keep in regular contact with your support network, updating them on your progress and any new challenges you're facing.

- **Reciprocal Support:** Be there for others in your support network when they need help. Supporting others can strengthen your relationships and provide a sense of purpose and connection.

- **Flexibility:** Your needs may change over time, so be open to adjusting how you engage with your support system. New resources or changes in your support network can bring fresh perspectives and strategies.

Conclusion:

Utilizing resources and support systems is a critical aspect of managing health-related anxieties effectively. By identifying helpful resources, building a supportive network, and staying engaged with your support system, you can enhance your ability to navigate healthcare experiences positively. Remember, managing anxiety is a journey that doesn't have to be undertaken alone—leveraging support and resources can make the path forward more manageable and successful.

13.4 Exercise: 10 MCQs with Answers at the End

Test your knowledge on creating a personal action plan for managing health-related anxieties, including setting realistic goals, monitoring progress, utilizing resources, and leveraging support systems.

Questions:

1. Setting realistic goals for managing health-related anxieties involves:

   A. Aiming for perfection in all healthcare interactions.

   B. Creating vague objectives to ensure flexibility.

   C. Using the SMART framework for clear, measurable targets.

   D. Focusing solely on long-term outcomes without interim milestones.

2. An effective strategy for monitoring progress in anxiety management is:

   A. Ignoring setbacks to maintain a positive outlook.

   B. Keeping a detailed journal of experiences and feelings.

   C. Setting unchangeable goals to stay on track.

   D. Avoiding feedback to prevent discouragement.

3. Utilizing digital tools for anxiety management can include:

   A. Meditation and mindfulness apps for daily practice.

   B. Online gaming to distract from anxiety triggers.

   C. Social media platforms for comparison with others.

   D. Avoiding technology to reduce stress.

4. A supportive network for managing health-related anxiety should ideally:

   A. Confirm your fears about healthcare settings.

   B. Offer empathy, shared experiences, and coping strategies.

   C. Discourage seeking professional help to build independence.

   D. Isolate yourself from potentially stressful interactions.

5. Regular review and reflection in managing health-related anxiety involve:

   A. Changing strategies daily to find what works best.

   B. Scheduling time to assess progress and adjust plans as needed.

   C. Sticking to the initial plan regardless of its effectiveness.

   D. Solely focusing on negative experiences for improvement.

6. Involving family and friends in your action plan for anxiety management means:

   A. Letting them handle all your healthcare decisions.

   B. Communicating your needs and how they can support you.

   C. Keeping your struggles private to avoid burdening them.

   D. Expecting them to understand your needs without communication.

7. Leveraging community and online resources for anxiety management can provide:

A. Instant cures for health-related anxieties.

B. Workshops, seminars, and support groups for learning and connection.

C. A platform for promoting self-diagnosis without professional consultation.

D. An opportunity to avoid real-life interactions and challenges.

8. Adapting your action plan for managing anxiety is essential because:

A. Initial plans are generally ineffective.

B. Anxiety levels and triggers remain constant over time.

C. It allows for the incorporation of new strategies and learning.

D. Professional advice should be disregarded in favor of personal intuition.

9. Celebrating achievements in your journey to manage anxiety helps by:

A. Ignoring smaller milestones in favor of significant successes.

B. Reinforcing positive behavior and maintaining motivation.

C. Focusing solely on the end goal without acknowledging progress.

D. Comparing your progress with others to gauge success.

10. Seeking professional guidance as part of your support system is crucial for:

   A. Outsourcing all responsibility for managing your anxiety.

   B. Gaining expert insights and strategies tailored to your needs.

   C. Following a standardized approach without personalization.

   D. Avoiding the development of personal coping mechanisms.

Answers:

1. C. Using the SMART framework for clear, measurable targets.

2. B. Keeping a detailed journal of experiences and feelings.

3. A. Meditation and mindfulness apps for daily practice.

4. B. Offer empathy, shared experiences, and coping strategies.

5. B. Scheduling time to assess progress and adjust plans as needed.

6. B. Communicating your needs and how they can support you.

7. B. Workshops, seminars, and support groups for learning and connection.

8. C. It allows for the incorporation of new strategies and learning.

9. B. Reinforcing positive behavior and maintaining motivation.

10. B. Gaining expert insights and strategies tailored to your needs.

These questions and answers underscore the importance of a comprehensive and adaptable approach to managing health-related anxieties, highlighting the role of realistic goal-setting, continuous self-reflection, leveraging a broad range of resources, and the value of a strong support network.

Chapter 14: The Psychological Impact of Chronic Illness

14.1 Dealing with Diagnosis

Receiving a diagnosis of a chronic illness can be a significant emotional and psychological turning point for many individuals. It often brings a mix of relief, understanding, and a sense of validation for symptoms experienced. Still, it can also trigger a range of complex emotions, including fear, anxiety, sadness, and anger. This subchapter explores strategies for managing the psychological impact of receiving a chronic illness diagnosis, aiming to provide guidance and support for navigating this challenging period.

Understanding the Emotional Response:

- **Normalizing Feelings:** Recognize that it is normal and valid to experience a wide range of emotions following a diagnosis. These feelings can fluctuate over time and may include stages of grief as you come to terms with the diagnosis.

- **Seeking Information:** Educate yourself about your condition through reputable sources. Understanding your illness can empower you and reduce feelings of helplessness and fear of the unknown.

Strategies for Coping:

- **Professional Support:** Consider seeking support from a mental health professional. Counseling or therapy can provide a space to process your emotions and develop coping strategies.

- **Peer Support:** Connecting with others who have the same or similar chronic conditions can provide comfort, understanding, and practical advice. Support groups, both in-person and online, can be invaluable resources.

- **Self-Care:** Prioritize self-care practices that promote physical and mental well-being. This can include regular exercise, a balanced diet, adequate sleep, and mindfulness or relaxation techniques.

Communication and Advocacy:

- **Open Communication:** Discuss your feelings and concerns with trusted family members or friends. Sharing your experiences can provide emotional relief and strengthen your support network.

- **Advocacy:** Become an advocate for your health by actively participating in decision-making about your treatment and care. Ask questions and express your needs and preferences to your healthcare providers.

Adjusting to a New Normal:

- **Setting Realistic Expectations:** Adjust your expectations to accommodate your health condition. This may involve redefining personal goals, modifying activities, and setting new priorities.

- **Maintaining Hope and Positivity:** Focus on what you can control and find ways to adapt. Cultivating a sense of hope and maintaining a positive outlook can significantly impact your mental health and quality of life.

- **Finding Meaning:** Many people find that their chronic illness journey leads them to discover new meanings and purposes in life. Engaging in activities that bring joy and fulfillment can contribute to a sense of well-being.

Long-Term Management:

- **Continuous Education:** Stay informed about new treatments, research, and management strategies for your condition. Ongoing education can help you make informed decisions about your care.

- **Lifestyle Adjustments:** Making lifestyle adjustments that accommodate your condition can help manage symptoms and improve your quality of life. This may include dietary changes, exercise modifications, and stress management techniques.

- **Monitoring Mental Health:** Be vigilant about monitoring your mental health. Chronic illness can increase the risk of depression and anxiety, making it essential to seek help if you notice significant changes in your mood or mental state.

Conclusion:

Dealing with the diagnosis of a chronic illness is a deeply personal and ongoing process. By employing effective coping strategies, seeking support, and actively participating in your care, you can manage the psychological impact and navigate the challenges that come with chronic illness. Remember, you are not alone, and resources and support systems are available to help you on this journey.

14.2 Mental Health and Chronic Disease

The intersection between mental health and chronic disease is significant and complex. Chronic diseases can significantly impact an individual's mental health, contributing to conditions such as depression, anxiety, and stress-related disorders. Conversely, mental health conditions can influence the course and management of chronic diseases, affecting outcomes and quality of life. This subchapter discusses the interplay between mental health and chronic disease, highlighting the importance of integrated care approaches to address both physical and psychological aspects of chronic illness.

Impact of Chronic Disease on Mental Health:

- **Psychological Burden:** Living with a chronic disease often involves coping with pain, fatigue, physical limitations, and uncertainty about the future, all of which can lead to feelings of despair, hopelessness, and isolation.

- **Increased Risk of Mental Health Conditions:** Studies show that individuals with chronic diseases are at a higher risk of developing mental health conditions, particularly depression and anxiety. The stress of managing a chronic condition can be a significant contributing factor.

- **Quality of Life:** The psychological impact of chronic disease can severely affect the quality of life, leading to decreased participation in social, recreational, and work activities.

Influence of Mental Health on Chronic Disease Management:

- **Adherence to Treatment:** Mental health conditions can affect an individual's ability to adhere to treatment regimens, including medication adherence, lifestyle changes, and attendance at medical appointments.

- **Disease Progression:** Poor mental health can influence the progression and management of chronic diseases. Stress, depression, and anxiety can exacerbate physical symptoms and complicate disease management.

- **Healthcare Utilization:** Individuals with co-existing chronic diseases and mental health conditions often require more healthcare services, leading to increased healthcare costs and utilization.

Integrated Care Approaches:

- **Collaborative Care Models:** Integrated care models that address both physical and mental health needs within the context of chronic disease management are essential. These models involve collaboration among healthcare providers, including primary care physicians, specialists, and mental health professionals.

- **Screening and Early Intervention:** Regular screening for mental health conditions in patients with chronic diseases allows for early identification and intervention, which can improve outcomes and quality of life.

- **Holistic Treatment Plans:** Treatment plans should consider both the physical and psychological aspects of chronic illness, incorporating strategies such as medication management, therapy, support groups, and lifestyle interventions.

Self-Management and Empowerment:

- **Education and Self-Care:** Educating patients about the link between mental health and chronic disease and empowering them to engage in self-care practices can enhance their ability to manage both aspects of their health.

- **Support Systems:** Encouraging patients to build and rely on support systems, including family, friends, and peer support groups, can provide emotional and practical assistance.

Conclusion:

The relationship between mental health and chronic disease underscores the need for a comprehensive approach to healthcare that addresses the full spectrum of patients' needs. Integrating mental health care into the management of chronic diseases can lead to better health outcomes, improved quality of life, and more efficient use of healthcare resources. Recognizing and treating mental health conditions as integral components of chronic disease care can significantly enhance patient care and well-being.

14.3 Strategies for Emotional Resilience

Emotional resilience is the ability to adapt to stress, adversity, or change, a critical skill for individuals dealing with chronic illnesses. Developing resilience can help mitigate the psychological impact of chronic disease, enhancing one's ability to navigate the challenges and uncertainties these conditions bring. This subchapter outlines strategies to build and strengthen emotional resilience, providing a foundation for better mental health and improved quality of life in the face of chronic illness.

Understanding Emotional Resilience:

- **Dynamic Process:** Emotional resilience is not a static trait but a dynamic process that involves behaviors, thoughts, and actions that can be learned and developed over time.

- **Individual Variation:** The path to building resilience varies among individuals, as personal experiences, support systems, and coping mechanisms influence it.

Key Strategies for Building Emotional Resilience:

1. **Maintain Social Connections:** Strong relationships with family, friends, and support groups can provide emotional support, practical assistance, and a sense of belonging, all of which are vital for resilience.

2. **Develop a Positive Outlook:** Cultivating optimism and maintaining a hopeful perspective can help manage the emotional challenges of chronic illness. Practice gratitude and focus on what is within your control.

3. **Accept Change:** Recognize that change is a part of life. Accepting circumstances that cannot be changed can help you focus on those you can influence.

4. **Set Realistic Goals:** Break down more considerable challenges into achievable goals. Accomplishing small tasks can boost your confidence and sense of mastery, fueling resilience.

5. **Take Decisive Actions:** Instead of detaching from problems and stresses, take decisive actions to address issues head-on, which can empower you and reduce feelings of helplessness.

6. **Prioritize Self-Care:** Engage in activities that enhance your physical, emotional, and mental well-being, such as regular exercise, adequate sleep, healthy eating, and mindfulness practices.

7. **Seek Purpose:** Engage in activities that bring meaning and joy to your life. This can include hobbies, volunteering, or work that feels significant to you.

8. **Embrace Healthy Thought Patterns:** Challenge and replace negative thoughts with more balanced and realistic thinking. Cognitive-behavioral strategies can be particularly effective in this regard.

9. **Learn from Experience:** Reflect on past challenges and how you overcame them. This reflection can enhance your understanding of your resilience and help you identify effective coping strategies.

10. **Seek Professional Help When Needed:** Don't hesitate to seek the guidance of mental health professionals if you're struggling to cope. Therapy can provide valuable tools for building resilience.

Implementing Resilience Strategies:

- **Personalized Approach:** Tailor resilience-building strategies to fit your personal preferences, lifestyle, and circumstances. What works for one person may not work for another.

- **Consistency:** Building resilience is an ongoing process that requires time and practice. Incorporate resilience strategies into your daily routine for maximum benefit.

Conclusion:

Developing emotional resilience is crucial for individuals facing the challenges of chronic illness. By adopting a proactive approach to building resilience, you can enhance your ability to cope with stress, recover from setbacks, and maintain a positive and fulfilling life despite the complexities of living with a chronic condition.

14.4 Exercise: 10 MCQs with Answers at the End

Test your understanding of the psychological impact of chronic illness, including dealing with diagnosis, the interplay between mental health and chronic disease, and strategies for building emotional resilience.

Questions:

1. Emotional resilience is best described as:

   A. A fixed trait that individuals are born with.

   B. The ability to avoid any form of stress or adversity.

   C. The capacity to adapt to stress and bounce back from adversity.

   D. Never experiencing negative emotions in response to stress.

2. an essential strategy for building emotional resilience is:

   A. Isolating oneself to avoid stressors.

   B. Maintaining strong social connections.

   C. Avoiding any changes to routine.

   D. Setting unattainably high goals for oneself.

3. Which of the following is a benefit of maintaining a positive outlook when dealing with chronic illness?

   A. Ignoring realistic aspects of the condition.

   B. Enhancing the ability to cope with emotional challenges.

   C. Guaranteeing a cure for the illness.

   D. Encouraging denial of the condition's seriousness.

4. Accepting change as part of life helps in building emotional resilience by:

   A. Preventing any adverse events from happening.

   B. Focusing on aspects of life that you can control.

   C. Eliminating the need for support or help from others.

   D. Ensuring that life remains constant and predictable.

5. The role of professional help in managing the psychological impact of chronic illness includes:

   A. Discouraging individuals from seeking any form of support.

   B. Providing tools and strategies to cope with stress and adversity.

   C. Promoting a sense of helplessness and dependency.

   D. Offering a temporary distraction from issues.

6. A realistic goal-setting strategy for someone with a chronic illness might involve:

A. Ignoring limitations imposed by the illness.

B. Achieving perfection in all aspects of life.

C. Breaking down more immense challenges into manageable tasks.

D. Setting goals that are impossible to achieve.

7. The impact of chronic disease on mental health can manifest as:

A. An immediate sense of relief and happiness.

B. Increased risk of developing conditions like depression and anxiety.

C. A decrease in the need for social interactions.

D. Enhanced physical health and well-being.

8. Engaging in self-care practices is crucial for:

A. Completely avoiding the reality of chronic illness.

B. Enhancing physical, emotional, and mental well-being.

C. Becoming entirely self-sufficient without any support.

D. Focusing solely on physical health while ignoring mental health.

9. Learning from past experiences to build emotional resilience involves:

   A. Dwelling on past failures and mistakes.

   B. Ignoring any lessons that could be learned from difficult times.

   C. Reflecting on how past challenges were overcome.

   D. Assuming that past successes guarantee future outcomes.

10. The integrated care approach to chronic illness emphasizes:

    A. Treating physical symptoms while ignoring psychological impacts.

    B. Addressing both physical and mental health needs.

    C. Focusing solely on medication as the solution to all problems.

    D. Separating mental health care from physical health care.

Answers:

1. C. The capacity to adapt to stress and bounce back from adversity.

2. B. Maintaining strong social connections.

3. B. Enhancing the ability to cope with emotional challenges.

4. B. Focusing on aspects of life that you can control.

5. B. Providing tools and strategies to cope with stress and adversity.

6. C. Breaking down more considerable challenges into manageable tasks.

7. B. Increased risk of developing conditions like depression and anxiety.

8. B. Enhancing physical, emotional, and mental well-being.

9. C. Reflecting on how past challenges were overcome.

10. B. Addressing both physical and mental health needs.

These questions and answers highlight the complexity of managing the psychological impact of chronic illness and underscore the importance of strategies for building emotional resilience, seeking support, and adopting an integrated care approach to navigate the challenges associated with chronic conditions.

Chapter 15: Preventative Strategies

15.1 Early Intervention Techniques

Preventative strategies play a crucial role in managing health conditions and mitigating the onset of chronic illnesses. Early intervention techniques are particularly effective in identifying risk factors, providing timely treatment, and preventing the progression of diseases. This subchapter explores various early intervention techniques that can contribute to maintaining health and preventing chronic illnesses.

Understanding Early Intervention:

Early intervention refers to the strategies and measures taken at the first signs of a health issue or when someone is at high risk of developing a condition. The goal is to address problems before they become more severe, reducing the risk of chronic illness and improving long-term health outcomes.

Key Early Intervention Techniques:

1. **Screening and Assessments:**

- Routine screenings for common health issues, such as high blood pressure, cholesterol levels, diabetes, and cancer, can detect problems early.

- Genetic screenings and assessments can identify individuals at high risk for certain conditions, allowing for proactive management.

2. **Lifestyle Modifications:**

- Encouraging a healthy diet, regular physical activity, adequate sleep, and stress management can prevent the development or progression of chronic diseases.

- Smoking cessation, reducing alcohol consumption, and avoiding substance abuse are critical components of preventing a wide range of health issues.

3. **Vaccinations:**

- Vaccines play a vital role in preventing infectious diseases that can lead to chronic health problems. Following recommended vaccination schedules can protect against various illnesses.

4. **Education and Awareness:**

- Providing individuals with information about risk factors, signs and symptoms of diseases, and healthy lifestyle choices can empower them to take control of their health.

- Public health campaigns and educational programs can raise awareness and promote behaviors that support health and well-being.

5. Mental Health Support:

- Early intervention in mental health can prevent the development of chronic mental health conditions. This includes access to counseling, stress reduction programs, and support for individuals showing early signs of mental health issues.

- Promoting mental health awareness and destigmatizing mental health care encourage individuals to seek help early.

6. Chronic Disease Management Programs:

- For individuals diagnosed with or at high risk for chronic conditions, participation in disease management or lifestyle intervention programs can prevent complications and improve quality of life.

- These programs often include education on managing the condition, medication management, and support for making lifestyle changes.

Implementing Early Intervention Strategies:

- **Collaboration with Healthcare Providers:** Working closely with healthcare providers to identify risk factors and implement appropriate screening and intervention strategies.

- **Personal Health Monitoring:** Individuals can use wearable technology and health tracking apps to monitor vital signs, physical activity, and other health metrics, providing valuable data for early intervention.

- **Community Resources:** Leveraging community resources, such as fitness programs, nutritional counseling, and mental health services, can support individuals in maintaining a healthy lifestyle and managing stress.

Conclusion:

Early intervention techniques are essential tools in the prevention and management of chronic illnesses. By identifying and addressing health issues early, implementing lifestyle modifications, and utilizing vaccinations and education, individuals and healthcare providers can work together to significantly reduce the risk of chronic disease and improve overall health outcomes.

15.2 Education and Outreach Programs

Education and outreach programs are pivotal components of preventative healthcare strategies. By raising awareness, providing accurate information, and encouraging healthy behaviors, these programs aim to empower individuals and communities to take proactive steps toward preventing chronic diseases and improving overall health. This subchapter delves into the various types of education and outreach programs, their objectives, and the impact they have on public health.

Types of Education and Outreach Programs:

1. **Public Health Campaigns:** These campaigns use media and public messaging to raise awareness about health risks such as tobacco use, obesity, and the importance of vaccinations, aiming to shift public attitudes and behaviors towards healthier choices.

2. **School-Based Health Education:** Programs implemented in schools educate children and adolescents about nutrition, physical activity, mental health, and substance abuse prevention, laying the foundation for lifelong healthy habits.

3. **Community Health Workshops:** Local health departments and organizations often host workshops and seminars on various health topics, including diabetes management, heart health, and cancer prevention, providing community members with valuable information and resources.

4. **Screening and Prevention Clinics:** Mobile clinics and community health events offer free or low-cost screenings for common health issues, such as high blood pressure, cholesterol, diabetes, and sexually transmitted infections, facilitating early detection and intervention.

5. **Digital Health Platforms:** Online platforms and mobile apps provide accessible health education materials, interactive tools for health assessment, and personalized recommendations for health improvement, reaching a broad audience.

Objectives of Education and Outreach Programs:

- **Increase Health Literacy:** Equip individuals with the knowledge needed to make informed decisions about their health and healthcare, improving their ability to navigate the healthcare system.

- **Promote Preventative Behaviors:** Encourage actions and lifestyle choices that can prevent the onset or progression of chronic diseases, such as adopting a healthy diet, engaging in regular physical activity, and abstaining from smoking.

- **Facilitate Early Detection:** Highlight the importance of regular health screenings and check-ups to identify health issues early when they are most treatable.

- **Reduce Health Disparities:** Target underserved and at-risk populations with tailored programs that address specific health disparities, aiming to improve health outcomes across all demographic groups.

Impact of Education and Outreach Programs:

- **Improved Public Health Outcomes:** Effective education and outreach can lead to reduced incidence of chronic diseases, lower healthcare costs, and improved quality of life for individuals and communities.

- **Empowered Communities:** By involving community members in health education efforts, individuals become advocates for their health and the health of their neighbors, fostering a culture of prevention and wellness.

- **Informed Healthcare Decisions:** With a better understanding of health risks and prevention strategies, individuals are more likely to engage in health-promoting behaviors and seek medical care when needed.

Conclusion:

Education and outreach programs are essential for advancing public health goals, preventing chronic diseases, and fostering a culture of health and wellness. Through diverse initiatives targeting individuals and communities, these programs play a critical role in improving health literacy, promoting healthy behaviors, and ultimately enhancing the health outcomes of populations worldwide.

15.3 Building a Culture of Understanding and Empathy in Healthcare

Creating a culture of understanding and empathy within healthcare settings is pivotal for enhancing patient care, improving health outcomes, and fostering a supportive environment for both patients and healthcare professionals. This culture shift towards empathy and understanding emphasizes the importance of seeing patients as individuals with unique experiences, values, and needs. This subchapter explores strategies for cultivating this culture and its impact on the healthcare experience.

Strategies for Cultivating Empathy and Understanding:

1. **Training and Education:** Implementing training programs for healthcare providers that focus on communication skills, emotional intelligence, and cultural competence can enhance their ability to connect with and understand patients on a deeper level.

2. **Patient-Centered Care Models:** Adopting care models that place the patient at the center of decision-making processes ensures that their preferences, values, and needs guide all aspects of care, promoting a more personalized and empathetic approach.

3. **Encouraging Narrative Medicine:** Encouraging healthcare professionals to listen to and value patients' stories and experiences can lead to a deeper understanding of the patient's perspective, fostering empathy and improving care.

4. **Building Diverse and Inclusive Teams:** Creating healthcare teams that reflect the diversity of the patient population can improve cultural competence

And I am understanding across the board. Diversity in healthcare providers can enhance patient trust, communication, and satisfaction by ensuring that patients feel seen, heard, and respected.

5. **Implementing Feedback Mechanisms:** Establishing effective channels for patient feedback allows healthcare institutions to understand patient experiences better and identify areas for improvement. Actively seeking and responding to feedback demonstrates a commitment to empathy and patient-centered care.

6. **Promoting Mental Health and Well-being Among Staff:** Healthcare professionals are better equipped to provide empathetic care when their mental and emotional well-being is supported. Initiatives that promote work-life balance, provide mental health resources, and address burnout can contribute to a more empathetic healthcare environment.

Impact of Empathy and Understanding in Healthcare:

- **Enhanced Patient Trust and Satisfaction:** A healthcare culture characterized by empathy and understanding can significantly enhance patient trust and satisfaction, leading to more positive healthcare experiences.

- **Improved Health Outcomes:** Patients are more likely to adhere to treatment plans and engage in proactive health behaviors when they feel understood and supported by their healthcare providers, leading to better health outcomes.

- **Reduced Healthcare Disparities:** A focus on empathy and understanding can help address healthcare disparities by ensuring that all patients, regardless of their background or circumstances, receive compassionate and equitable care.

- **Increased Job Satisfaction Among Healthcare Professionals:** Working in an environment that values empathy and understanding can lead to higher job satisfaction and morale among healthcare staff, reducing turnover and fostering a positive work environment.

Conclusion:

Building a culture of understanding and empathy in healthcare is essential for delivering high-quality, patient-centered care. By implementing strategies that promote empathy, encourage patient-centered care models, and support the well-being of healthcare staff, healthcare institutions can create an environment where patients feel valued and understood. This cultural shift not only improves patient experiences and outcomes but also contributes to a more satisfying and rewarding work environment for healthcare professionals, ultimately leading to a more effective and compassionate healthcare system.

15.4 Exercise: 10 MCQs with Answers at the End

This exercise aims to reinforce critical concepts related to preventative strategies in healthcare, including early intervention techniques, the role of education and outreach programs, and the importance of building a culture of understanding and empathy within healthcare settings.

Questions:

1. Early intervention techniques in healthcare are designed to:

    A. Address health issues only after they become severe.

    B. Detect and address health issues before they progress.

    C. Focus solely on treatment, not prevention.

    D. Discourage patients from participating in their care.

2. A key component of public health campaigns is:

    A. Promoting unhealthy lifestyle choices.

    B. Decreasing public awareness about health issues.

    C. Using media to raise awareness and encourage healthy behaviors.

    D. Ignoring the importance of vaccinations.

3. School-based health education programs primarily aim to:

    A. Discourage physical activity among students.

    B. Lay the foundation for lifelong healthy habits.

    C. Limit students' understanding of mental health.

    D. Promote the use of tobacco and alcohol.

4. Vaccinations play a crucial role in:

   A. Increasing the prevalence of infectious diseases.

   B. Preventing infectious diseases that can lead to chronic health problems.

   C. Discouraging public health initiatives.

   D. Reducing the need for healthcare services.

5. Emotional intelligence training for healthcare providers helps to:

   A. Decrease their understanding of patient needs.

   B. Improve communication and empathy towards patients.

   C. Encourage a dismissive attitude towards patients' emotions.

   D. Focus solely on technical skills.

6. Patient-centered care models prioritize:

   A. The healthcare provider's convenience over patient needs.

   B. The patient's preferences, values, and needs in care decisions.

   C. A one-size-fits-all approach to treatment.

   D. Minimizing direct communication with patients.

7. The primary goal of narrative medicine is to:

   A. Ignore patients' stories and experiences.

   B. Encourage healthcare professionals to listen to and value patients' narratives.

   C. Discourage empathy in medical practice.

   D. Focus only on clinical data and symptoms.

8. Mental health support for healthcare staff contributes to:

   A. Increased burnout and job dissatisfaction.

   B. A more empathetic healthcare environment.

   C. Decreased quality of patient care.

   D. Ignoring the well-being of healthcare professionals.

9. Cultural competence in healthcare is essential for:

   A. Promoting misunderstandings between providers and patients from different backgrounds.

   B. Providing equitable and respectful care to all patients.

   C. Decreasing the effectiveness of communication.

   D. Excluding diverse perspectives in healthcare delivery.

10. Effective patient feedback mechanisms are used to:

    A. Dismiss patient concerns and experiences.

    B. Identify areas for improvement in patient care.

C. Discourage transparency within healthcare settings.

D. Limit patient involvement in their care.

Answers:

1. B. Detect and address health issues before they progress.

2. C. Using media to raise awareness and encourage healthy behaviors.

3. B. Lay the foundation for lifelong healthy habits.

4. B. Preventing infectious diseases that can lead to chronic health problems.

5. B. Improve communication and empathy towards patients.

6. B. The patient's preferences, values, and needs in care decisions.

7. B. Encourage healthcare professionals to listen to and value patients' narratives.

8. B. A more empathetic healthcare environment.

9. B. Providing equitable and respectful care to all patients.

10. B. Identify areas for improvement in patient care.

These questions emphasize the significance of early intervention, education, outreach, and the cultivation of empathy and understanding in healthcare to improve patient outcomes and experiences.

Conclusion

As we conclude our exploration of the multifaceted world of healthcare, it's clear that managing health-related anxieties, preventing chronic illnesses, and creating a supportive and empathetic healthcare environment is crucial for enhancing patient care and outcomes. From understanding the psychological impact of chronic disease to implementing preventative strategies and fostering a culture of empathy, the journey through these topics highlights the importance of a holistic approach to healthcare.

Key Takeaways:

- **Managing Health-Related Anxieties:** Strategies such as early intervention, personalized care plans, and leveraging support systems are vital for individuals navigating health-related anxieties, including White Coat Syndrome.

- **Preventative Strategies:** Early detection, education, outreach programs, and lifestyle modifications play critical roles in preventing chronic illnesses and promoting overall well-being.

- **Empathy and Understanding in Healthcare:** Cultivating a culture of empathy and understanding within healthcare settings is essential for providing patient-centered care, enhancing communication, and building trust between patients and healthcare providers.

- **Emotional Resilience:** Building emotional resilience is crucial for individuals dealing with chronic illness, allowing them to adapt to stress, overcome challenges, and maintain a positive outlook on life.

- **Integrated Care Approaches:** Addressing both the physical and psychological aspects of health through integrated care approaches leads to better health outcomes and improved quality of life for patients.

Moving Forward:

The insights and strategies discussed underscore the importance of a comprehensive approach to healthcare that considers the physical, psychological, and emotional needs of patients. By prioritizing prevention, early intervention, and the development of supportive healthcare environments, we can work towards a future where healthcare is more accessible, effective, and compassionate.

Healthcare professionals, patients, and communities alike have roles to play in this journey. Through collaboration, education, and continuous improvement, we can create a healthcare system that not only treats illness but also promotes health, resilience, and well-being for all individuals.

Conclusion:

The exploration of these topics serves as a reminder of the complexity of healthcare and the importance of addressing it holistically. By fostering understanding, empathy, and resilience and by implementing effective preventative and management strategies, we can hope to see a future where healthcare is not just about treating diseases but about nurturing overall health and well-being.

*The best way to thank an author is
to
write a review.*

Printed in Great Britain
by Amazon